# Town Trails

## North Yorkshire

### Mark Reid

A selection of 25 walks through
the towns and cities of North Yorkshire

InnWay Publications

**Town Trails**
*North Yorkshire*

© Mark Reid 2001

First Edition July 2001
Reprinted October 2001

A catalogue record for this book is available from the British Library.
British Library Cataloguing in Publication Data.

The contents of this publication are believed correct at time of copyright.
Nevertheless the author can not accept responsibility for errors and omissions,
or for changes in details given. The information contained within this publication
is intended only as a general guide. Walking and outdoor activities can be
strenuous and individuals must ensure that they have suitable clothing, footwear,
provisions and are suitably fit before starting the walk.

*Published by:*
INNWAY PUBLICATIONS
102 LEEDS ROAD
HARROGATE
HG2 8HB


ISBN   1 902001 06 0

# Contents

*This book is dedicated to the many kind and helpful people of the towns of North Yorkshire.*

I am extremely grateful to the following people and organisations who have helped with my research: Beck Isle Museum, Beech End Model Village, City of York Council, Craven District Council, English Heritage, Green Howards Regimental Museum, Hambleton District Council, Harrogate Borough Council, Mrs Peacock of Middleham, North Yorkshire County Council, North Yorkshire Moors Railway, Richmondshire District Council, Richmond Georgian Theatre, Richmondshire Museum, Ripon Spa Hotel, Ryedale District Council, Scarborough Borough Council, www.streetmap.co.uk, The National Trust, Yorkshire Tourist Board, Upper Wharfedale Folk Museum, Valerie Taylor of Easingwold, Wensleydale Railway Association.

Thank you also to Bernadette and Stewart Reid, Rachel Gospel and Matthew Hunt for accompanying me on many of the walks.

*This project has been supported by the North Yorkshire Foot and Mouth Disease Fund.*

# Introduction

Researching this book has been a revelation. Despite growing up in North Yorkshire and knowing, or so I thought, all of the towns and cities in this, England's largest county, familiar places I thought I knew well have been given fresh, new life. Market towns, coastal resorts and cathedral cities have taken on new dimensions. Hidden amongst the streets, lanes and alleyways of these twenty-five towns is a wealth of beautiful architecture, fascinating history, legend and folklore waiting to be discovered; and all at a gentle walking pace.

Armed with a little knowledge, these towns come alive with history and interest for here you will find the largest Gothic cathedral in Northern Europe, England's most historic Spa Town, a Norman castle beneath which King Arthur and his Knights lie asleep, the Roman town of Isurium Brigantium, a fishing village that was once the 'smuggling capital of the North', the highest market town in Yorkshire, James Herriot's surgery and the port from where Captain Cook set sail on his journeys of discovery.

The many bustling market towns offer a wealth of individual shops, traditional crafts and family owned businesses that sell a wide range of local quality produce that is becoming harder to find in the increasingly homogenous High Street. This, coupled with numerous traditional Yorkshire inns and tea rooms, will ensure your visit is made even more enjoyable.

You are guaranteed a warm and friendly welcome from the people of North Yorkshire.

# Useful Information

| | |
|---|---|
| **WEBSITE:** | http://www.innway.co.uk |
| **PUBLIC TRANSPORT:** | National Express bookings: 0990 808080<br>Rail enquiries: 08457 484950<br>*There are Railway Stations at: Harrogate, Knaresborough, Malton, Northallerton, Scarborough, Settle, Skipton, Thirsk, Whitby and York. Pickering is served by the North Yorkshire Moors Railway.* |
| **GENERAL BUS AND TRAVEL INFORMATION:** | Metroline (West Yorkshire): 0870 608 2 608<br>Travel-line York: 01904 551400 |
| **ORGANISATIONS:** | English Heritage: 01904 601901<br>Yorkshire Regional Office<br>37 Tanner Row<br>York<br>YO1 6WP<br>*Website:* www.english-heritage.org.uk<br><br>The National Trust: 01904 702021<br>Yorkshire Regional Office<br>27 Tadcaster Road<br>York<br>YO24 1GG<br>*Website:* www.nationaltrust.org.uk<br><br>North Yorkshire County Council: 01609 780780<br>County Hall<br>Northallerton<br>DL7 8AD<br>*Website:* www.northyorks.gov.uk |

North York Moors National Park Authority:
01439 770657
The Old Vicarage
Bondgate
Helmsley
North Yorkshire
*Website:* www.northyorkmoors-npa.gov.uk

Rambler's Association: 020 7339 8500
Camelford House
87-90 Albert Embankment
London
SE1 7TW
*Website:* www.ramblers.org.uk

Yorkshire Dales National Park Authority:
01756 752748
Hebden Road
Grassington
North Yorkshire
*Website:* www.yorkshiredales.org.uk

Yorkshire Tourist Board: 01904 707961
312 Tadcaster Road
York
*Website:* www.yorkshirevisitor.com

**WEATHER INFORMATION:**

Weathercall: 09068 505 318
*Information supplied by the Met Office.*
*Premium Rate calls.*

**GENERAL ADVICE:**

Whilst undertaking these Town Trails please remember to:
- Keep to public Rights of Way
- Respect private property and gardens
- Take litter home and clean up after your dog
- Take care crossing roads, railway lines and bridges
- Arrive properly prepared with suitable clothing and footwear
- Protect your skin against direct sunlight

# Bedale

| | |
|---|---|
| **TIME:** | One & a half hours |
| **START:** | Bedale Market Cross in the Market Place. |
| **TOILETS:** | Car Park off Bridge Street |
| **CAFÉ:** | The Farmhouse Teashop or The Courtyard Tea Rooms in the Market Place. |
| **PUBS:** | Six to choose from: the Waggon and Horses, The Green Dragon, The White Bear, Old Black Swan and The King's Head in the Market Place or The Three Coopers on Emgate. |
| **PARKING:** | Two large car parks off Bridge Street. |
| **INFORMATION:** | Bedale Tourist Information Centre: 01677 424604. |
| **MARKET DAY:** | Tuesday |

> *"The wide cobbled Market Place sweeps gracefully through the heart of this old North Riding market town, at the centre of which is an ancient stepped Market Cross - there has been a weekly market here since Henry III granted the town a Market Charter in 1251."*

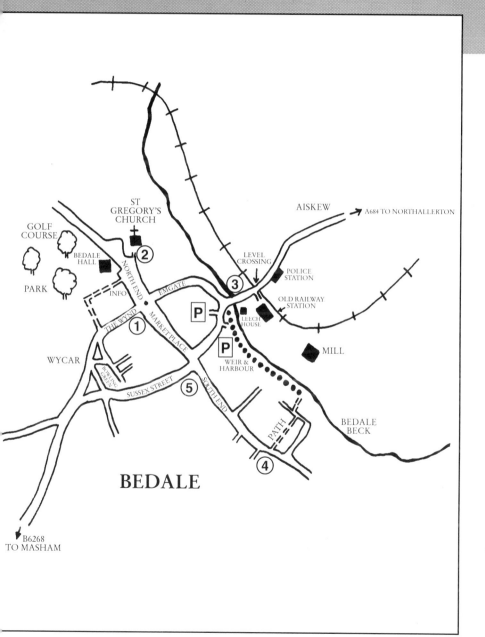

BEDALE

**1.** *From the Market Cross in the centre of the Market Place walk up along the left-hand side of the street (North End) to reach Bedale Hall, then cross the road to St Gregory's Church.*

The history of Bedale can be traced back to Saxon times, when a small settlement grew around the point where the ancient routes from Ripon, Northallerton and Wensleydale converged. The wide cobbled **Market Place** sweeps gracefully through the heart of this old North Riding market town lined with many fine Georgian buildings, old coaching inns and interesting shops, at the centre of which is an ancient stepped **Market Cross** - there has been a weekly market here since Henry III granted the town a Market Charter in 1251. As you walk towards Bedale Hall note the row of exquisite three-storey Georgian houses including the well-proportioned 'Stabann'. These houses date from the 18th Century at a time when the town's prosperity grew during the height of the coaching era. Through the archway on the left are a range of old houses and stabling blocks that were built during the late 18th Century by the Peirse family of Bedale Hall who went on to develop a successful racing stud with winners in prestigious races such as the St Leger; this archway once formed part of the old Coach Road to Lancaster. **Bedale Hall** is an imposing Georgian house noted for its fine plasterwork. For many years it was the home of the Peirse family who had bought the Manor of Bedale in the 17th Century from the descendants of the Fitzalan family. The Peirse family built a small manor house here during the 1650's, which was subsequently enlarged in 1730 into the house we see today. The Hall was requisitioned for the Armed Forces during the Second World War, however when the army moved out in 1948 squatters moved in and it fell into disrepair. The local District Council bought the Hall in 1951 and began restoration and it is now owned by Hambleton District Council and houses the library and a small museum of local life. Beyond the house across the playing fields is a small mound covered with trees below which is an 18th Century **Ice House,** an important facility for wealthy families before refrigerators were invented. **St Gregory's Church** has been a site of worship since Saxon times, however the present church dates from the 12th to 14th Centuries. The Church is noted for its 14th Century mural of S George and the Dragon as well as four stone effigies including that of Brian Fitzalan Lord of Bedale, who fought alongside Edward I and died in 1306. Lady Chapel was built in the 13th Century and is noted for its large window known as the Jervaulx Window. This is said to have taken its name from a chantry endowed for the monks of Jervaulx Abbey to pray for souls of the Fitzalan family, although some authorities claim that the window actually came from Jervaulx Abbey following the Dissolution of the Monasteries - it does appear to be far too big for the wall in which it is housed. The tower is a rare example of a fortified tower that was built in the early 14th Century due to the threat of Scottish raids; a portcullis once protected the doorway leading up into the tower. The small stone cottage in the churchyard (dated 1674) was once the **Old Grammar School** before a 'new' Grammar School was built across the own at Wycar in 1888. There had been a Free Grammar School in Bedale since Medieval times, however it fell into disuse only to be re-established by Elizabeth I in 1588.

Jan A. Aos 101.

2. *Walk out of the Church and head back down through the Market Place then turn left at the Market Cross along Emgate. Follow this down bending round to the right to reach the road junction with Bridge Street (adjacent to Bedale Bridge).*
As you walk down through the Market Place you pass Plummers Wine Bar on your left, named after the builder who rebuilt it in 1716 (note the drainpipe '1716 TP'). **Emgate** is an ancient thoroughfare where the town's craftsmen once lived. The **Three Coopers** is said to date back to the 16th Century and is reputedly haunted. A detour to the left across **Bedale Bridge** takes you up to the railway station, level crossing and signal box of the **Wensleydale Railway**. This railway reached Bedale from Northallerton in 1855 and opened fully between Northallerton and the Settle to Carlisle Railway at Garsdale in 1878, however the line closed for passenger services in 1954. The tracks were kept between Northallerton and Redmire to service quarries

and, more recently, to transport M.o.D. equipment to the ranges above Wensleydale. The Wensleydale Railway Association was formed in 1990 to try to re-establish the link to Garsdale and resume passenger services along the existing track - services look set to resume as far as Leyburn with plans to extend the line to Aysgarth and eventually all the way to Garsdale.

**3.** *At the Bridge cross over the road and head along the riverside path directly opposite, which quickly takes you to a weir and the Harbour. Continue straight on alongside the river for approximately 200 yards then turn right up some steps along an enclosed path passing between the houses and onto a road in a housing estate. Turn left here then turn right along another enclosed path just before the road bends round to the right and follow this up to join the main road.*

Look downstream of Bedale Bridge and you will see a small brick-built house known as the **Leech House,** a unique survivor from the days when blood-sucking leeches were an integral part of medical practice. Leeches were stored in this building from the late 18th Century up until the early 1900's and were used by local practitioners who believed that they helped to relieve 'congestion' for almost any ailment ranging from headaches to inflammation. This listed building was restored in the 1980's after many years of neglect. A very pleasant path leads down alongside **Bedale Beck** - look out for the overgrown millstream that slants off to the left and once provided power for **Aiskew Mill,** an old watermill that produced flour and animal feed until it closed in 1968. This mill has found a new lease of life as a visitor attraction producing cheese and ice cream and has rare breed poultry and pigs. You soon come to a weir in an area known as the **Harbour.** During the mid 18th Century there was an ambitious scheme to make Bedale Beck navigable to the River Swale to connect with the River Ure down to Boroughbridge. This canal basin was constructed, complete with iron rings to secure the boats, and the river straightened for some distance, however a lack of resources meant that the project was never completed.

**4.** *Turn right along the main road and follow this up back towards the main Market Place (South End). As you enter the Market Place turn left at the crossroads along Sussex Street.*

As you walk back toward the Market Place, note the large stone Victorian building on your left with its three-storey central portion and two wings. This was originally built as a poor house and later used as a hospital; it has since been converted into flats. Spend some time exploring the **South End** of the Market Place with its many Georgian buildings, old inns and traditional shops. Along the left-hand side of the Market Place, known as Top Flags, there are a number of fine three-storey Georgian coaching inns including the King's Head, Waggon and Horses and the Green Dragon with a number of interesting shops sandwiched in between, many still with their original Victorian frontages. Along Lower Flags buildings of note include the old Town Hall, which dates from 1840 and still retains its original large sash windows or the second floor whilst further along is the Old Black Swan with its original 18th Century façade.

**5.** *Walk up along Sussex Street then at the crossroads turn right and follow this road down passing the Bowling Green to reach a T-junction. Turn right here passing the small 'green' and then the Methodist Chapel on your right and continue straight on along The Wynd back to the Market Place.*

The well-kept bowling green is used by the **Bedale Bowling Green Society,** which was established in 1792 making it one of the oldest in England. This part of Bedale is known as **Wycar,** originally a separate settlement that still retains its own character. The focal point of this area is the delightful triangular 'green' protected by posts and chains with an old water pump under a canopy. Attractive houses surround the green including a number of large Victorian houses as well as an ornate mock-Tudor building complete with a Royal Coat of Arms. This was the old **Grammar School,** which originally stood in the churchyard and was rebuilt here in 1888, although it is now a private house. Our route continues along **The Wynd** passing the Bedale Methodist Church and then a row of old cottages on the left, complete with a working gunsmiths.

# Boroughbridge & Aldborough

## ⓘ ESSENTIAL WALK INFORMATION

**TIME:** Three hours

**START:** Main car park off the High Street in the centre of Boroughbridge.

**TOILETS:** Situated in the main car park.

**CAFÉ:** Bygones Tea Rooms along the High Street.

**PUBS:** Several to choose from; try the Crown Hotel, the Three Horse Shoes or the 13th Century Black Bull at Boroughbridge also The Ship Inn at Aldborough.

**PARKING:** Large car park off the High Street.

**INFORMATION:** Boroughbridge Tourist Information Centre: 01423 323373

> *"The Devil's Arrows stand as one of the 'Great Wonders of Yorkshire'; three huge prehistoric monoliths of millstone grit that are shrouded in mystery and legend."*

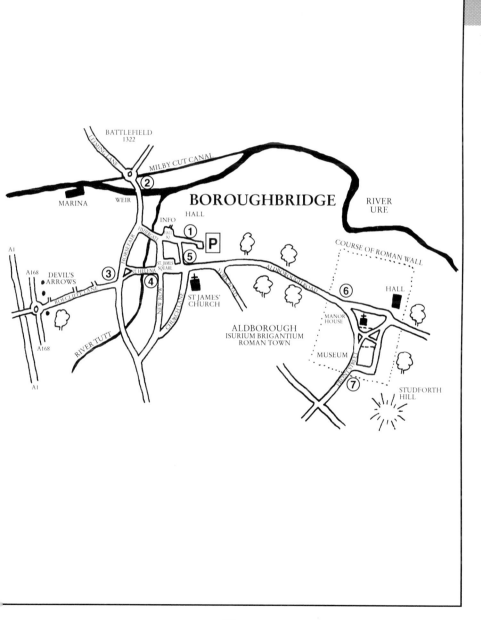

*1. Leave the main car park in the centre of Boroughbridge along the road passing Hall Square on your right to quickly reach the road junction at the bottom of High Street. Head straight on along Fishergate then at the T-junction turn right along Horsefair and follow this to reach the bridge over the River Ure.*

**Hall Square,** sometimes referred to as the Market Square, is a picturesque cobbled square at the centre of which is a War Memorial surmounted by a white statue of peace. Overlooking the square is a row of whitewashed houses originally built as fishermen's cottages, whilst to the right is a covered veranda that once served as the butter market - the town was granted a Market Charter in 1310 by Edward II. The imposing gates, with their fine wrought ironwork, lead to **Boroughbridge Hall** where Isabella Bird, later Mrs Bishop, was born in 1831, a famous explorer, missionary and author. The main road that passes along Horsefair down to the bridge across the River Ure was part of the **Great North Road** (A1) until the by-pass was opened in 1963 - for almost one thousand years this was the main route between the North and South. The **Crown Hotel** stands proudly in the heart of the town, an old coaching inn dating back to the 17th Century that once boasted stabling for over 100 horses. During the town's heyday in the 18th Century there were twenty-two inns to quench the thirst of the countless drovers, travellers, tradesmen and stagecoach passangers that came this way. The Roman Road of **Dere Street** forded the River Ure half a mile downstream at Milby, however following the Norman Conquest this road was improved with the construction of a wooden bridge at Boroughbridge, heralding the development of the town; the bridge was rebuilt in stone in the 16th Century. This was the site of the **Battle of Boroughbridge** in 1322 when King Edward II's army, commanded by Sir Andrew Harcla, defeated the rebel forces of the Earls of Lancaster and Hereford. Hereford was killed by a sword thrust up through the bridge whilst Lancaster sought refuge in St James Church only to be dragged from the altar and subsequently beheaded. A short walk over the river into Langthorpe brings you to the canal, known as the **Milby Cut.** This stretch of canal was built in 1773 as part of a series of works that included five locks as well as short sections of canal which connected Ripon and Boroughbridge with the English canal network via the rivers Ure and Ouse. The canal made Boroughbridge a thriving port carrying flax for the Knaresborough linen industry. The construction of the Darlington to York Railway in 1841 heralded its decline and by 1894 it was silted up and dilapidated. The Ripon Canal Society was formed in 1983 and has since renovated and restored the canal - it is now used by pleasure craft with moorings and a marina.

*2. Retrace your steps back across the bridge into the centre of Boroughbridge. Head straight on along Horsefair passing the Post Office and Forge House on your right to reach the turning on the right (Roecliffe Lane).*

As you walk back along **Horsefair** note the Three Horse Shoes on your right, one of the oldest pubs in the town that has been in the same family since around 1900. It was rebuilt in the 1930's and remains completely unaltered offering a unique glimpse o how pubs used to be. Just after the Post Office, with its old signs for Money Order Office and Post Office Savings Bank, is a fine Georgian house at **No. 3 Horsefair** complete with original railings, bow windows and old gas lamp. Further along the road, opposite the Crown Hotel, is a large Georgian building with a sign depicting three greyhounds, once the home of the Mauleverer family whose crest included these dogs; the house later became a coaching inn known as the **Three Greyhounds.** At one time it also incorporated a tailors shop, which was owned by the family of Captain Archie White of the 6th Battalion The Yorkshire Regiment who won the Victoria Cross in 1916 for his bravery on the Western Front. Continue along Horsefair passing **Forge House,** an old blacksmith's shop with its metal wheel hoop still set into the pavement. This would have been a very busy place years ago as Horsefair, as the name implies, was where regular horse markets and fairs were held.

**3.** *Turn right along Roecliffe Lane and follow this out of the town to reach the Devil's Arrows in a field on your right near the busy A1(M). Retrace your steps back along Roecliffe Lane to reach the junction with Horsefair where you take the lane opposite to the left (St Helena). Follow this road down over a bridge across the River Tutt and on to the junction with New Row in the corner of St James Square.*

**The Devil's Arrows** stand as one of the 'Great Wonders of Yorkshire'; three huge prehistoric monoliths of millstone grit that are shrouded in mystery and legend. It is thought that they were dragged here from Plumpton near Knaresborough around 2,700 BC although another story tells us that they were thrown by the Devil at the town. No one really knows what purpose they served and why they are set in a line, although they almost certainly had some religious significance - there were originally four, possibly five, Arrows. **St Helena** opens out into an attractive square, one of three market squares in the town. **Peggy Bridge** spans the River Tutt providing access to St James Square; it is said that the fourth Devil's Arrow was used to build this bridge. **The Black Bull** stands on the corner of New Row and St James Square, an ancient inn that dates back to the 13th Century.

**4.** *Turn right along New Row and follow this road up out of the town, then take Church Lane to the left (opposite the playground) almost back on yourself and follow this down into St James Square.*

**New Row** is an attractive street of brick-built cottages with old yards, smallholdings and stabling behind. **St James' Church** originally stood in St James Square between the Fountain and the Library but was demolished in 1851 and rebuilt on its present site with only a few fragments of the original Norman church incorporated into the new building. **St James Square** is a delight with an assortment of Victorian, Georgian and older cottages lining the cobbled square, at the centre of which is the **Fountain** beneath an ornate canopy. The pump, given to the town by Mrs Lawson of Aldborough Manor, dates from 1875 and draws water from a depth of 256-ft. It is said to be the deepest well in the country.

John A.Ives '01.

**5.** *From St James Square head out of the town along Aldborough Road then take the turning on the left as the main road swings round to the right and follow this road for half a mile into Aldborough.*

**Aldborough** is a fine country village with stone cottages surrounding a large village green, however beneath the quiet lanes and gardens are the walls of one of Rome's great urban settlements as Aldborough stands on the site of the Roman town of **Isurium Brigantium.** Founded in the 2nd Century AD it was one of a score of towns established after the Roman invasion as a centre of government and administration to rule over the local population. Isurium Brigantium lay at the centre of the lands previously controlled by the Brigantes, the largest of the native British tribes. The town also protected the river crossing where Dere Street forded the River Ure and was well defended with stout stone walls over 12-ft high with four large entrance gates enclosing an area of 55 acres. It would have been a splendid place with luxurious villas and many public buildings including a large forum, baths and temples. The Roman town was abandoned in the early 5th Century AD and was subsequently ransacked by invading Danes and Vikings in the 9th Century. When the river crossing was moved upstream to Boroughbridge, the 'Old Borough' became a small farming village much as it is today. As you walk into the village you pass **Aldborough**

**Manor,** a large Georgian manor house. Note how the road rises outside the front door and then continues as a ridge across the field to the left - this was the site of the West Gate with the Roman Town Wall running northwards. There are many Roman remains in the gardens of Aldborough Manor (private) including a section of Town Wall and the bathhouse. The stone monument on the small 'green' ahead of you is the **Battle Cross,** erected after the Battle of Boroughbridge in 1322 and moved here in 1852 from Hall Square.

**6.** *As you enter the village and the road divides - head straight on along the left-hand branch passing between the pub and the church and follow the road round to the right then at the triangular 'green' turn right up to reach the main village green. Continue straight on along Back Street and follow it up and round to the right to reach Front Street.*

**St Andrews Church** stands on the site of the Roman forum and a temple dedicated to Mercury - a carved relief statue of Mercury was found in the 14th Century and incorporated into the north-west wall of the church. This church was rebuilt in 1330 to replace a Norman structure that had been destroyed by the Scots in 1318; the tower dates from the 15th Century and is almost certainly built from Roman stones. Inside, the church is an architectural gem noted for its brass of William de Aldeburgh which dates from around 1360, probably the oldest such brass in Yorkshire. The focal point of the village is the village green with its tall maypole. At the top of the green stands the **Old Court House** where MPs were elected until 1832 for the ancient borough of Aldborough and Boroughbridge, once a 'Rotten Borough'. There is also a memorial to the crew of a Royal Canadian Airforce Lancaster bomber that crashed in 1944 killing the seven crewmen - the pilot managed to bravely avoid the village crashing instead into **Studforth Hill.** This hill lies just to the south of Aldborough and is claimed to be the site of Roman gladiatorial battles! Where Back Street meets Front Street there is a fascinating **English Heritage Museum** housing displays of Roman pottery, coins and artefacts, sections of the Town Walls and the famous Lion and Star Mosaics.

**7.** *Turn right down along Front Street passing the village green again on your right, then follow the road as it bears down to the left to join Aldborough Road again which you follow back into Boroughbridge.*

**Front Street** was once the main road into the Roman town from the south and still follows the line of the Roman Road. Note the old Victorian Methodist Chapel on your right with its colourful stained glass windows and further along the road just before the green is the old village blacksmith's shop. Further down along the road you pass Aldborough Post Office and Dairy, a lovely building with an old AA sign attached to the wall with distances to Aldborough from towns and cities including London.

# Easingwold

**TIME:** One & a half hours

**START:** Market Cross, Easingwold Market Place.

**TOILETS:** Beside the old Town Hall in the Market Place

**CAFÉ:** Clark's Tea Rooms in the Market Place.

**PUBS:** Several to choose from; try the George Hotel or the Angel Inn.

**PARKING:** Free Car Park along Crabmill Lane off the main Market Place.

**INFORMATION:** Easingwold Tourist Information Centre: 01347 821530

**MARKET DAY:** Friday

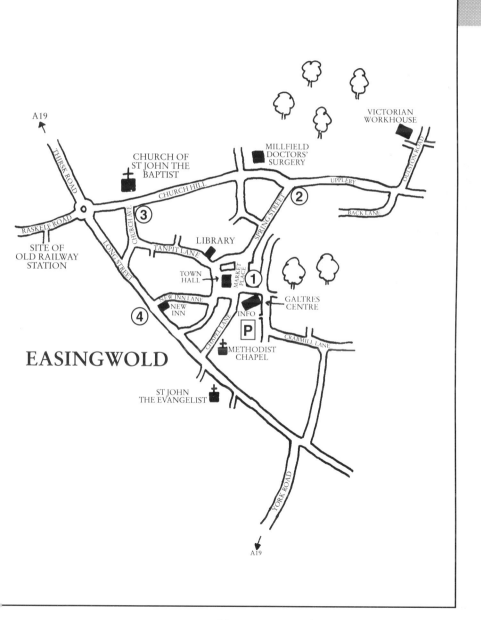

**1.** *From the Market Cross in the centre of the Market Place, head up along the road passing the War Memorial on your left out of the top right-hand corner of the Market Place along Spring Street. Follow this up to reach the road junction at the top of the street in Uppleby.*

Easingwold was once a busy staging post on the old coach road North from York and still retains an air of prosperity with many fine Georgian houses surrounding the attractive Market Place. The name of the town is probably derived from 'ease' meaning fertile land and 'wold' meaning forest, although some sources suggest that 'easing' may have been a personal name. Following the Norman Conquest Easingwold began to develop as a trading centre in the middle of the Forest of Galtres, a vast hunting forest frequented by the nobility of York; the forest had all but disappeared by the 17th Century. The slightly haphazard layout of the **Market Place** is a delight with many elegant Georgian and Victorian houses, shops and old coaching inns overlooking a cobbled market place, at the centre of which is a stepped **Market Cross** beneath an ornate shelter. There has been a market held in the town since at least 1221, although the Crown held the rights to the market and the local men had to pay for the 'privilege' by giving the King a horse! The weekly Friday market dates from 1638 when the Market Charter was granted to George Hall, a local landowner. Just to the north of the Market Cross are two circular designs in the cobbles, the larger one marks the site of the old bull-ring whilst the smaller one was where pigs were tethered on market day. The old **Town Hall** dominates the Market Place, a fine building that dates from 1864. It stands on the site of the 17th Century 'shambles' or butchers stalls, derived from the old English word 'shamel' which refers to the benches once used to display meat; it is now home to a firm of printers. In front of the Town Hall is a small 'green' protected by railings with a **Victorian Drinking Fountain** placed there in 1883 as a tribute to John Haxby by his widow. Buildings of note include the **George Hotel,** an 18th Century coaching and posting inn, whilst the three-storey Georgian building to its right was once the York Union Bank. Overlooking the War Memorial is the **White House,** perhaps the finest building in the town and a wonderful example of Georgian architecture with bold overhanging eaves and a well-proportioned façade. Note the house almost hidden to your right, with its old fashioned lettering above the front door "Chapman, Medd & Sons, Est. 1865, Cabinet Makers & Funeral Directors, Tel Eas 370". **Spring Street** boasts a number of interesting buildings including Charles Hobson Outfitters Shop that was once a pub known as the Malt Shovel, whilst on your left is the single-storey **Victoria Buildings** of 1897, which originally served as the community centre until The Galtres Centre opened. You pass a small cottage on your right with the inscribed datestone above the door of 'God With Us 1664', for this was a half-timbered cottage before it was rebuilt in 1907. Nearby is a roadside stone where you can still see the small stream running underground that gave the street its name. This stream skirts to the north of the Market Place and can also be seen along the side-road opposite where there is an old drinking trough. Across the road to the left is **Blayds House,** built in 1840 originally as a Primitive Methodist Chapel.

**2.** *Follow the road round to the right through Uppleby down to reach the crossroads with Oulston Road. Retrace your steps along the other side of the street back to reach the road junction at the top of Spring Street. Take the turning to the right along Church Hill (to 'Thirsk, Boroughbridge') and follow this up to reach the Church.*

An old 'North Riding of Yorkshire' signpost points along the tree-lined street of **Uppleby** with rows of old brick cottages set back behind a wide grassy verge. This was originally a separate village and still retains its own character. It was first settled in the 10th Century by a Danish farmer called 'Upple' literally on the doorstep of the neighbouring Anglo-Saxon settlement of Easingwold. A short detour up along Oulston Road takes you to the old **Victorian workhouse,** built in 1837 some distance from the town - out of sight, out of mind perhaps? The small half-timbered **Tudor House,** probably the oldest house in the town, stands at the junction of Spring Street and Church Hill. As you walk up along Church Hill, the area to the right now occupied by the Doctors' Surgery, was where the old **Archdeaconry Manor House** stood until it was demolished in 1826. This was an ecclesiastical manor of around 40 acres that provided income for the cleric. There has been a manor house on this site since at least 1201 when it belonged to the King, however ownership passed to the

Archdeacons of Richmond in 1269 with whom it stayed until the 16th Century when it passed to the Bishops of Chester and finally to the Archbishop of York in 1974. This ecclesiastical manor was quite different from the much larger civil Manor of Easingwold and Huby given to Robert de Mowbray following the Norman Conquest. **The Church of St John the Baptist and All Saints** has been a site of worship since Anglo-Saxon times, however the first stone church was built following the Norman Conquest. Only a Norman capital from a pillar remains of this early church as it was entirely rebuilt between 1388 and 1418, although the tower was added in the 15th Century. The spacious interior boasts an unusual Victorian balcony, a 15th Century stone cross shaft, a rare 17th Century Parish coffin and a charity linen box. The grave of Ann Harrison lies in the churchyard near the Chancel door, a former landlady of the Blue Bell Inn in Uppleby who, according to her unusual epitaph, had a sharp tongue, bad temper and a fist she didn't mind using!

**3.** *Turn left along Church Avenue opposite the main entrance to the Church then where this lane divides follow the left-hand branch (Tanpit Lane) back down into the Market Place. Walk straight on across the Market Place, keeping to the right-hand side of the road, then head along Little Lane out of the corner of the Market Place, taking the turning almost immediately on the right (New Inn Lane). Follow this down through the yard of the New Inn to reach Long Street.*

Easingwold was once a major centre for shoemaking during the 18th and 19th Centuries, with 28 cobblers in the town. The Old Tannery along **Tanpit Lane** provided the raw materials for this industry, however this workshop closed in the early 1900's and has since been converted into a house. Just as you enter the Market Place you pass **Easingwold Library** which is housed in the old Easingwold National School, built in 1862 with the rather stern inscription of 'Learn or Leave' above the door. Across the road to the right is the **Old Vicarage,** a fine Georgian house built in 1777 to replace an earlier house that had been destroyed by fire. This side of the Market Place is an absolute delight with beautiful Georgian houses and cottages overlooking cobbled forecourts and a wide grassy verge. Of particular note is **Rocliffe House,** a wonderful brick-built late 18th Century house that was once the home of Dr Rocliffe in the 19th Century who, it is said, was a keen supporter of cock-fighting and even had a cockpit in the house!

**4.** *Turn left along Long Street then take the second turning to the left along Chapel Lane and follow this up back into the Market Place.*

It was during the 18th and 19th Centuries that Easingwold enjoyed great prosperity as the town was the first stop for stagecoaches on the road North from York; **Long Street** formed part of the A19 until the by-pass was built in the 1990's. A number of old coaching inns remain including the **New Inn** with its coaching arch and stabling yard at the rear; there were once 26 inns to slake the thirst of travellers in the late 18th Century. On the corner of Long Street and Little Lane stands the impressive three-storey **Longley House,** a former coaching inn known as the New Rose and Crown before it became a convent in 1905; it has since been converted into flats. The arrival of the railway in 1891 heralded the terminal decline of the coaching era. This railway was a privately owned branch line that connected the town to the main line at Alne, the last of its kind when it finally closed for passengers in 1948 and freight in 1957; the old Station Hotel can still be seen just off Raskelf Road. Long Street still retains much of its character with many fine houses, shops and pubs lining a wide street, which opens out after the turning for Little Lane with grassy verges and trees. Note the old milepost in the verge for Easingwold with distances to London (209 miles) and York (13 miles). Our route turns to the left here along Chapel Lane, however further along Long Street to the right is the **Catholic Church of St John the Evangelist,** a fine stone church built in 1830 and designed by Charles Hansom, whose brother Joseph designed the famous Hansom cab. **Easingwold Methodist Church** is situated along Chapel Lane, a 1970's building that replaced an earlier chapel that had been built in 1815 although there has been a Wesleyan Methodist Church on this site since 1786. Note the solitary gravestone hidden amongst shrubs of John Skaife who died in 1838 aged 73, one of the first preachers of Methodism in the town. As you walk back into the Market Place you pass **The Galtres Centre** on your right, which was built in 1897 as a private house on the site of another large house. The building had stood empty and neglected for many years before Hambleton District Council bought it in the early 1980's and began restoring the house; it now houses the Easingwold Community Centre, Council Chambers and sports facilities. Note the old gateposts with the inscription to the 'Army and Navy of Great Britain and Ireland MDCCCIX', which commemorate the Peninsula War of 1809 - 1814.

# Grassington

**TIME:** Two hours

**START:** National Park Car Park along Hebden Road.

**TOILETS:** Yorkshire Dales National Park Visitor Centre Car Park or Linton Falls car park.

**CAFÉ:** Several to choose from including Cobblestones Caf overlooking The Square.

**PUBS:** Four to choose from: the Black Horse Hotel, Foresters Arms, Devonshire Hotel or the Grassington House Hotel.

**PARKING:** Large Yorkshire Dales National Park Car Park along Hebden Road.

**INFORMATION:** Yorkshire Dales National Park Visitor Centre, Grassington: 01756 752774

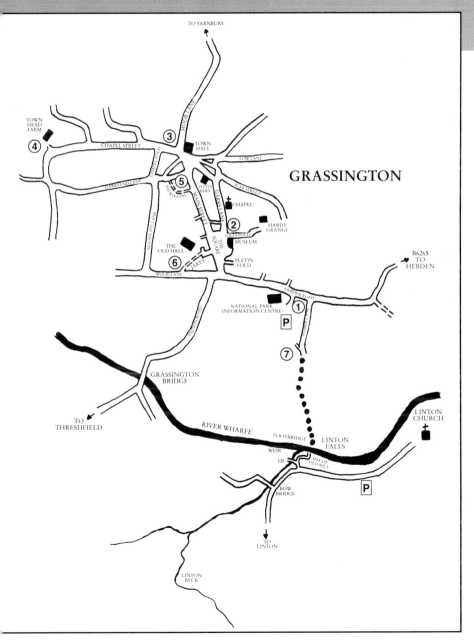

GRASSINGTON

1. *From the main car park beside the Yorkshire Dales National Park Visitor Centre head left along Hebden Road towards the town centre. Where the road swings round to the left take the turning to the right and walk up into The Square, keeping to the right-hand side, to reach Garrs Lane in the far right-hand corner.*

Grassington is an attractive small town set in the heart of Wharfedale, a popular tourist destination due to its picturesque cobbled square, stone cottages and winding alleyways that beckon you to explore. As you turn along Main Street into The Square you pass an old blacksmiths' shop known as **The Smithy**, the last of four that once served the town. Across to your left is **Church House**, a wonderful example of a 17th Century yeoman's farmhouse built by Stephen and Alice Peart in 1694 as the inscription above the door recalls. It is now used as a place of worship for the people of Grassington as the Parish Church lies some distance away across the River Wharfe. **The Square** opens out before you offering a wonderful view up across the cobbled market place lined with an assortment of old cottages and Georgian buildings. Grassington developed as a trading centre in the forest of Wharfedale as it lay on two important routes, the monastic road from Fountains Abbey to the Lake District and the road from Skipton to Wensleydale. The town was granted a Market Charter in 1282 which secured its status as the 'capital of the upper dale', however regular markets lapsed in the late 19th Century. To your right is **Pletts Fold,** one of many back lanes to be found throughout the town known locally as 'folds' that were originally crofts in-filled with cottages over the centuries. **Cobblestones Café** and Moore's China Shop are housed in a row of old stone cottages, which possibly date back to the 17th Century, in front of which is a good example of an old drain and gutter with three holes drilled through a piece of rock set in the cobbles. Overlooking The Square is the **Upper Wharfedale Folk Museum**, which houses a fascinating display of local artefacts, old farming implements, lead mining displays plus much more. Hidden away along **Gills Fold** is Scar Lodge, an elegant three-storey house attached to which is one of Grassington's most historic buildings. **Hardy Grange** (private) is thought to have belonged originally to the monks of Fountains Abbey who held grazing lands in this area and who also brought large flocks of sheep this way between Fountains Abbey and their monastic farms, otherwise known as 'granges'; the present building is largely 17th Century.

2. *Walk up along Garrs Lane passing the Black Horse Hotel. At the top of this lane just before it bends round to the left and Scar Street turns off to the right, take the rough lane to the left. Follow this track down passing Pletts Barn and up to reach the Town Hall at the top of Main Street.*

Just off Garrs Lane to the right is the imposing **Black Horse Hotel,** a fine old 17th Century coaching inn with a wonderful open fireplace. You soon come to the **Grassington Congregational Church,** which dates from 1811 and is still in use, a simple building with an attractive interior. The house opposite the entrance to the churchyard is **Theatre Cottage,** which originally formed part of a barn where theatre was housed in the early 19th Century upon whose boards Edmund Kean once trod. The rough lane that leads off Garrs Lane, known locally as **Water Lane,** is thought to follow the line of the Roman Road between Ilkley and Bainbridge. Hidden away off this lane is **Pletts Barn,** a wonderful example of a 17th Century stone-built barn with exquisite details including dovecotes and a cobbled forecourt where John Wesley once preached in the late 18th Century. **Grassington Town Hall** and Devonshire Institute stands at the top of Main Street, built in 1855 originally as a Mechanics Institute but given to the new Parish Council by the Duke of Devonshire in the late 19th Century. It was extended in the 1920's and again in 1998 to provide more modern facilities for theatre, festivals and exhibitions. **Moor Lane** leads to the side of the Town Hall up to Yarnbury and the wild moors beyond. This was once a major lead mining area, particularly during the 18th and 19th Centuries, though by the early 1900's mining had virtually ended due to cheaper imports.

**3.** *From the Town Hall head along Chapel Street and follow this all the way down to reach Town Head Farm.*
The cobbled lane that leads off Main Street just to the left of Chapel Street is **Chamber End Fold,** a picturesque lane lined with attractive 17th Century stone cottages. The large three-storey house on the corner with its weathered inscription dates from the 18th Century and is said to have once housed the local court's 'chamber', hence the name of this lane. As you might expect, there are a number of old chapels along **Chapel Street** including the old Primitive Methodist Chapel of 1837 just off to the left along Chapel Fold. Further along Chapel Street is Grassington Methodist Church, which dates from the early 19th Century and is still used for worship. A number of old lead miners' cottages are passed before you come to **Town Head Farm,** one of the town's finest buildings and a superb example of a 17th Century Dales farmhouse with stone mullion windows and a protruding two-storey porch. This farm belongs to the Trustees of the Fountaine Hospital at Linton and provides revenue for Fountaine Hospital almshouses.

**4.** *At Town Head Farm continue along the lane and follow it down to the left into open countryside. You soon reach a fork in the road at a small triangular 'green', turn left here along Garrs End Lane and follow this heading back into Grassington. This lane soon divides - bear left along Garrs End Lane (ignore Moody Sty Lane to the right) to reach Main Street again.*
**Garrs End Lane** leads from the town centre towards Grass Wood and the site of the original village of Grassington. There is evidence of a large Iron Age settlement at Lea Green above Grass Wood, however the first village was established by Anglo-Saxon settlers around the 7th Century to the west of the town. This was abandoned in the 12th Century when the Manor was transferred from the Percys to the Plumptons and the present-day town established. Garrs End Lane gives an insight into the origins of the name of the town as it is thought that a Saxon farmer called Garr settled in this area and cleared an enclosure or 'tun'.

**5.** *Turn right down along Main Street back into The Square then turn right after Woodware (adjacent to The Pump) along a passageway (signpost to 'Grassington Lodge'). This quickly opens out into a small courtyard, follow the enclosed path (known as 'Jakey') ahead that bends round to the left and follow this down to reach Wood Lane.*

As you emerge onto Main Street from Garrs End Lane, note the old stone drinking troughs outside **Craven Cottage** and Wellhead Cottage opposite. A small stream once ran down this street, which was originally called Well Lane; it now flows through a culvert. Further down along Main Street on the right is the **Dales Kitchen,** which was once the chemist's shop of John Crowther during the 1880's. Crowther was a keen collector of local artefacts and established Grassington's first museum in a small wooden shed near the Town Hall. When he died in 1930 most of his exhibits went to the Craven Museum at Skipton. An ancient Right of Way known as **The Woggins** leads to the side of the Dales Kitchen and emerges along Garrs End Lane. The small building on the right that now houses a gallery was once a blacksmith's shop owned by **Tom Lee** in 1766, Grassington's most infamous criminal. Lee was a notorious highway robber who murdered Dr Petty in Grass Wood after he had threatened to expose his mischievous ways. Lee was later hanged at York and his body gibbeted in Grass Wood. The row of Georgian buildings overlooking The Square to your left, which now house Country Concept and Rowan, are known as the **Liverpool Warehouse.** In Victorian times this building became a shop that sold a selection of quality goods that came from Liverpool by canal; it was the 'Selfridges of the Dales'. In the centre of The Square is **The Pump,** otherwise known as the Fountain, a recently restored water pump that supplied the town's drinking water in the 19th Century. Look out for the circular stone set into the cobbles nearby which once had a ring used to tether bulls for baiting. An old passageway, known as **Jakey,** leads from The Square down to Wood Lane, passing alongside the boundary wall of the **Old Hall** (private), said to be the oldest inhabited house in Yorkshire. The house dates back to the 13th Century when it was built for Robert de Plumpton as his hunting lodge. The Plumptons were Lords of the Manor until the 16th Century and had links with the monks of Fountains Abbey - it is said that there is a secret underground passage between here and Hardy Grange.

**6.** *Turn left along Wood Lane down to the road junction with Station Road, where you retrace your steps back along Hebden Road to the car park.*

Station Road leads down to the right to cross the River Wharfe by way of **Grassington Bridge,** a fine stone structure that dates from the 17th Century. The railway arrived at Grassington in 1902 (the station was situated just across the bridge) and helped develop the tourist industry. The line closed for passenger services in the 1930's, although it is still open to freight traffic serving Swinden Quarry to the south of Threshfield.

**7.** *Detour: A spectacular end to this walk takes in the delights of Linton Falls and Linton Church. Take the footpath that leads out of the bottom left-hand corner of the Car Park and follow this walled path down over the footbridge above Linton Falls, then skirt to the right around the houses to reach the road. Turn left here and follow the lane down to Linton Church. Retrace your steps back to the car park.*

A walled path, known as the Snake Walk, takes you down across a footbridge above **Linton Falls,** an impressive sight after heavy rain when the River Wharfe tumbles over rocks caused by the Craven Fault. Note the weir and old mill race which once provided power for **Linton Mill** before it closed in 1959. A mill has stood on this site since medieval times, however the old mill building was demolished and new houses built in the 1980's, although some millworkers' cottages remain. **Linton Church,** dedicated to St Michael and All Angels, has a lovely setting beside the Wharfe and dates from Norman times, although much altered in the 14th and 15th Centuries. It is built in characteristic Dales' style and still serves the surrounding villages of Grassington, Hebden, Threshfield and Linton from where ancient paths lead to the church.

# Harrogate

| | |
|---|---|
| **TIME:** | Two hours |
| **START:** | The Cenotaph in the centre of Harrogate. |
| **TOILETS:** | Victoria Shopping Centre |
| **CAFÉ:** | Plenty of choice: try Betty's on Parliament Street or the Magnesia Well Café in the Valley Gardens. |
| **PUBS:** | Several to choose from; try the Old Bell Tavern on Royal Parade, Hales Bar on Crescent Road or the Coach and Horses on West Park. |
| **PARKING:** | On-street parking throughout the town. |
| **INFORMATION:** | Harrogate Tourist Information Centre: 01423 5373 |

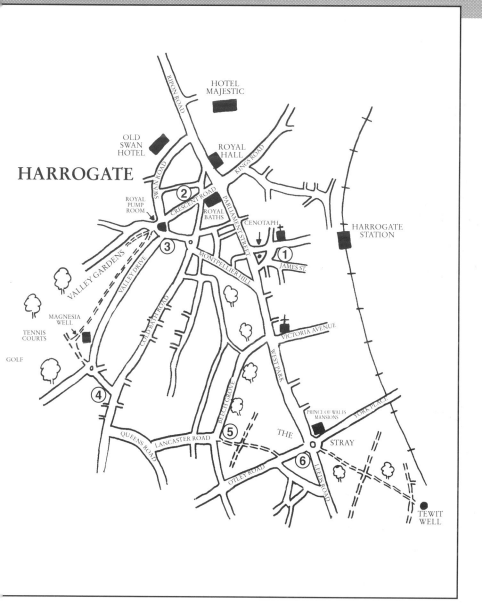

# HARROGATE

For centuries Harrogate was little more than a hamlet in the Forest of Knaresborough, indeed the name of the town is derived from 'Herehlaw-gate' meaning 'the road to Harlow Hill'. However, in 1571 the discovery of a mineral spring known as Tewit Well changed the fortunes of the town forever and England's first Spa Town was born. Other springs were soon discovered and the town began to flourish during the 18th Century as a resort for wealthy people to come and 'take the waters'. Inns and lodging houses were built around the Old Sulphur Well and along the edge of the Forest common land, which was later to form The Stray. Harrogate's heyday was during the 19th and early 20th centuries when it became a fashionable Spa Town with an unrivalled social life for well-heeled visitors. The fortunes of the Spa began to decline during the inter-war period and by the 1950's many of the old Spa buildings had closed. The town has since reinvented itself as an exhibition and conference centre.

1. *From the Cenotaph in the centre of Harrogate, head down along Montpellier Parade passing Betty's Café on your right down to reach the roundabout in front of The Crown Hotel. Turn right here along Montpellier Road to reach Crescent Road with Crescent Gardens in front of you.*

**The Cenotaph** soars skyward in the heart of Harrogate, a memorial to the local men who gave their lives during the two World Wars. It is framed on two sides by **Prospect and Cambridge Crescents,** stunning examples of bold Victorian architecture created by George Dawson, Harrogate's most famous property developer. **Betty's Tea Rooms** was first established in 1919 and is still a family business, famed for its mouth-watering displays of cakes, as well as its own blend of tea and roasted coffee - a visit to this Yorkshire institution is a 'must'. Montpellier Hill is a delightful sweep of beautiful gardens overlooked by some of the finest shops in the town. A short detour along Montpellier Street takes you to **Montpellier Mews** in the heart of the Antiques Quarter with dozens of shops and dealers - this complex of old stone cottages was once stables and garages for the town's many Bath Chairs. **Farrah's Harrogate Toffee** shop can be found along Montpellier Parade. This famous toffee was first made in 1840 and includes lemon oil, designed to take away the taste of the sulphur water. The **White Hart Hotel,** with its wonderfully proportioned façade stands proudly at the foot of Cold Bath Road and was built in 1847 to replace a smaller coaching inn. **The Crown Hotel** was established in the 17th Century as a small inn adjacent to the Old Sulphur Well, however the reputation of the hotel grew quickly and it became popular with wealthy visitors. The Thackwray family owned the hotel during the 18th and early 19th Centuries and transformed it into Low Harrogate's finest hotel. The central portion of the present building dates from 1847 with the two 'wings' added on some twenty years later. On the corner of The Ginnel is **White Cottage,** a small building that was once the ticket office of the Montpellier Baths and Gardens. During the 1820's numerous sulphur springs were discovered in this vicinity and in 1834 a luxurious suite of baths, surrounded by gardens, were built by Mr Thackwray of The Crown. In 1869 this Estate was bought by George Dawson who improved the facilities, however all of the buildings were demolished in 1897 to make way for The Royal Baths.

**2.** *Turn left along Crescent Road passing Crescent Gardens on your right to reach the Royal Pump Room Museum with Valley Gardens ahead of you.*

When **The Royal Baths** opened its doors in 1897 it was hailed as the most advanced centre for hydrotherapy in the world. Sadly, The Royal Baths closed for treatment in 1969 except for the Turkish Baths, which still provide a taste of the Victorian splendour for which Harrogate was once so famous. The Royal Baths complex has recently been redeveloped with bars, restaurants and improved facilities at the Turkish Baths. Across to the right is **The Royal Hall,** built in 1903 to provide entertainment for the visitors to the Spa. The **Royal Spa Concert Rooms** originally stood to the south of The Royal Hall, a magnificent Classical building constructed in 1835 with a façade of six Doric columns beneath a large portico. It was demolished in 1939 and the land redeveloped for the 'new' exhibition trade. In 2000 a striking new exhibition hall was built on the site, a good example of sympathetic architecture reminiscent of the old Spa Rooms. All around here are large hotels including the **Hotel Majestic,** a lavishly appointed hotel of immense proportions that opened in 1900, and the Hotel St George that began life as a humble lodging house in the 18th Century. Across from The Royal Baths are the offices of Harrogate Borough Council, housed in the former **New Victoria Baths** building of 1871, converted to its present form in 1931. In front of this building are **Crescent Gardens,** laid out in the 1890's as an amenity for visitors. The gardens take their name from an old inn known as the Half Moon that previously stood on the site. Crescent Road leads up towards the entrance to Valley Gardens passing **Hales Bar** on your right, a wonderful example of a Victorian public house still with its original gas lighting. A short detour along Swan Road to your right takes you to The **Mercer Art Gallery.** This was built in 1806 by public subscription as the Promenade Rooms where visitors could socialise after 'taking the waters'. Dominating this road is the **Old Swan Hotel,** which dates back to the early 18th Century. In 1926 Agatha Christie famously 'disappeared' for eleven days and was found by reporters here. The cobbled lane behind the Royal Pump Room is known as **Crown Place,** and was the scene of one of Harrogate's most famous incidents when in 1835 Thackwray, the owner of The Crown Hotel, tried to divert the public sulphur wells for his own use. This caused outrage amongst the town's business people who relied on the public wells for their livelihoods. The Harrogate Improvement

Commissioners were subsequently formed whose main objective was the improvement of the public wells. Their first task was to replace the old stone canopy above the Old Sulphur Well with an elegant copper-domed **Royal Pump Room** in 1842 - the glass and iron annexe was built in 1913 to ease congestion during the morning rush when up to 1,500 glasses of sulphur water would be served. The Royal Pump Room closed after the Second World War and now houses a fascinating museum. A tap outside provides a free supply of mineral water but be warned as this is the strongest sulphur well in the world, in constant use since the 17th Century!

John A. Ives '00.

**3.** *Walk up through the Valley Gardens, keeping to the left-hand lower path passing the Magnesia Well Pump Room to reach the tennis courts and play area. Turn left here, through the gates and onto the road by a small roundabout. Head along Valley Drive opposite that quickly leads up to a T-junction with Cold Bath Road.*

The **Valley Gardens** are the jewel in the crown of Harrogate's gardens, a wonderful swathe of mature trees and plants set around a small stream that winds its way down from Harlow Hill. This area was originally a footpath across fields between the Bogs Field and the Old Sulphur Well, however the adjoining land was bought by the Council during the late 19th Century and the gardens laid out for visitors to enjoy. Our route alongside the stream is known as the **Elgar Walk,** as Edward Elgar was a regular visitor to Harrogate between 1912 and 1927. Up to your right is the **Sun Colonnade and Sun Pavilion,** which were opened in 1933 to provide a covered walkway. The buildings finally closed in 1982 after years of neglect but were fully restored and re-opened by the Queen in 1998. The ornate **Magnesia Well Pump Room** was built in 1895 to replace the Old Magnesia Well, a small pump room built in 1858 by the Improvement Commissioners which can be found across to your right hidden by trees. This area is known as the **Bogs Field** and actually forms part of The Stray, protected by the Award of 1778. Within this area thirty-six of Harrogate's eighty-eight mineral springs rise to the surface, each one of which is different making this area globally unique. Until the 1850's these springs trickled away into the surrounding marshy ground, hence the name of Bogs Field.

**4.** *Turn right along Cold Bath Road then take the turning to the left along Queen's Road. As this road sweeps round to the right, head left along Lancaster Road and follow this down to reach Beech Grove and The Stray.*

**The Stray** surrounds the heart of Harrogate and provides over 200 acres of open parkland for people to enjoy. This sweep of open land once formed part of the vast common lands of the Royal hunting Forest of Knaresborough. During the 18th Century there were moves to enclose much of the open land and commons of England, however in the years that followed the Enclosure Act of 1770 fears grew over public access to Harrogate's mineral wells. An Award of 1778 set aside over 200 acres of the old common land to ensure open and free access to the mineral springs. This Award stated that The Stray should *"for ever remain open and unenclosed and all persons whomsoever shall and may have free access at all times to the said springs and be at liberty to use and drink the waters there arising."*

**5.** *At Beech Grove walk along the footpath opposite that heads across The Stray, bearing slightly to the right, to join Otley Road. Turn left to quickly reach the Prince of Wales Roundabout at the junction with Leeds Road, York Place and West Park.*

As you approach the Prince of Wales Roundabout look across to your right towards

Trinity Methodist Church. This triangular section of The Stray was the site of Harrogate's first railway station, known as **Brunswick Station,** which opened in 1848. It formed the terminus of a line that ran from Church Fenton on the main Leeds to York line, however the station closed in 1862 when another railway was built through the heart of the town. The arrival of the railway heralded a new era in the development of Harrogate. Estates of large townhouses and villas began to be built throughout the town for wealthy commuters; these stand today as some of the finest planned Victorian housing developments in the world. **West End Park,** the area of land between Otley Road and Leeds Road, was developed during the 1870's and boasts many opulent mansions facing onto The Stray. **The Prince of Wales Mansions** date back to 1815 when a small lodging house known as Hattersley's Hotel was established on this junction of the Leeds to Ripon Turnpike. Extended and enlarged during the late 19th Century, the hotel became known as the Prince of Wales, however it was converted into flats during the 1950's.

**6.** *At the Prince of Wales Roundabout, cross Leeds Road and head diagonally across The Stray to your right along the footpath shaded by mature trees down to reach Tewit Well. Retrace your steps back to the roundabout then head along West Park down to reach the Cenotaph.*

The history of Harrogate's Spa began in 1571 when William Slingsby stopped his horse beside a spring on the common land of the Forest of Knaresborough - he had been attracted to it by a flock of lapwings, known locally as tewits, that were drinking from it. Slingsby was a well-travelled man from a wealthy local family and noticed the similarity of this spring water to those of the town of Spa in Belgium. He informed Dr Bright, physician to Elizabeth I, of his discovery - this was the first place in England to be referred to as a 'spa'. Before long, the reputation of these 'medicinal' waters grew to almost 'cure all' status. The stone canopy that shelters **Tewit Well** dates from 1807 and originally covered the Old Sulphur Well before the Royal Pump Room was built. After 400 years of use Tewit Well, England's most historic Spa, was closed in 1971. Just along West Park is a large stone that marks the boundary of the **Leeds to Ripon Turnpike** that came through the town in the 18th Century. Numerous coaching inns were built along West Park including the **Clarendon Hotel,** a fine Georgian inn situated just after the Prince of Wales Mansions of which only a small portion survives above the shopfronts. After the **West Park Hotel,** known as The Commercial when it was established in the early 19th Century, and before the junction with Victoria Avenue, is a fine terrace of Regency houses. **Victoria Avenue** was the showpiece of the Victoria Park Company, which was founded in 1860 by Messrs Carter, Ellis and Richardson who bought up the farmland between High and Low Harrogate (much of the present-day town centre) to build estates of high-class houses. Note the flamboyant **Belvidere House** on the corner of the road, the first house to be built in 1861. Further along West Park is **Cathcart House,** where the Czarina of Nicholas II stayed when she came to visit the Spa. Just before you reach the cenotaph again, you pass the **Imperial Hotel** (formerly the Prospect Hotel) on your right, which dates back to 1814 when it was a small lodging house.

# Hawes & Gayle

**TIME:** Two & a half hours

**START:** Yorkshire Dales National Park Centre, Burtersett Road.

**TOILETS:** National Park Centre Car Park or the Market Place

**CAFÉ:** Several to choose from; try Laburnum House along The Holme or the Wensleydale Creamery Visitor Centre.

**PUBS:** A choice of four: The Crown, Fountain Hotel, White Hart Inn and the Board Hotel.

**PARKING:** Pay & Display car park adjacent to the National Park Centre and The Ropemakers.

**INFORMATION:** Yorkshire Dales National Park Centre, Hawes: 01969 667450

**MARKET DAY:** Tuesday

> *"Mossy Haw Lane affords wonderful views of Upper Wensleydale and the surrounding hills that cradle the town - across to the right a narrow strip of tarmac climbs steeply out of Sleddale over Fleet Moss to a height of 589m, the highest road in Yorkshire."*

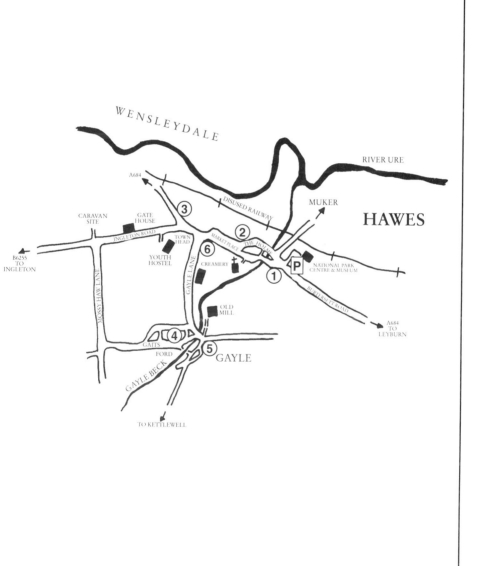

1. *From the large Car Park (Station Yard) beside the National Park Centre, Dales Countryside Museum and The Ropemakers, walk up to the main road where you turn right. Follow this road ('No Entry' road signs) over Holme Bridge and up along The Holme into the bottom of the Market Place.*

Hawes lies at the head of Wensleydale, the highest market town in Yorkshire at 850ft above sea level - 'hawes' is thought to be derived from the Old Norse word for a mountain pass. First mentioned in 1307, it remained little more than a clearing in the forest for many centuries, however the increasing packhorse trade along routes that converged at Hawes meant that the town was granted a Market Charter in 1699, taking over from Askrigg as the market for the upper dale. The Lancaster to Richmond Turnpike came this way in 1795 and then the railway arrived in the 1870's, which opened up new markets for local stone, agricultural and dairy products as well as bringing in tourists. Hawes was the terminus of the North Eastern Railway's Wensleydale line from Northallerton which opened in 1878. From here the railway linked up with the Midland Railway Company's Settle to Carlisle Railway via a branch line from Hawes Junction - **Hawes Station** is a classic example of Midland Railway's 'Derby Gothic' architecture. The railway closed for passengers in 1954 and freight in 1964, though there are efforts to reopen the line. **The Dales Countryside Museum** is housed in the old Station buildings and large Goods Shed and tells the story of the people of the Dales and how the landscape has evolved over the centuries. Across from here are the workshops of **W. R. Outhwaite & Sons**, Ropemakers, one of the last remaining independent ropemakers in the country. This business was founded in the mid 19th Century by Mr Wharton and was taken over by W. R Outhwaite in 1905, who moved from Gate House along the Ingleton Road to the present site in 1922. It remained in the Outhwaite family until 1975 when Peter and Ruth Annison took over. As you reach the main road you pass a small graveyard on your right sheltered by old yew trees - this is an old **Quaker burial ground** dating back to around 1680. **Holme Bridge** was built in 1956 to ease traffic congestion through the narrow streets and over the old stone bridge. The road soon opens out into an area known as The Holme, a name derived from the old Norse word meaning a flat meadow - it is thought that this area was the site of the original settlement.

2. *Walk up along the right-hand side of the Market Place to reach Dalehead Garage at Town Head.*

The ornate **Barclays Bank** building to your right was originally a branch of the Wensleydale and Swaledale Banking Company, whose head office was at Richmond with branches at Bedale, Leyburn and Hawes; the company was bought by Barclays in 1899. There are a number of older cottages sandwiched between the Victorian and Georgian inns and hotels that line the main street including **Cockett's Hotel,** which is housed in a 17th Century cottage with an inscription above the door of "Ano Dom 1668 God being with us who can be against TAF". This was once a resting house for Quakers visiting the town as well as destitute travellers; the initials are those of

Thomas Fawcett, a local Quaker. **Littlefairs,** a traditional ironmongers and builders' merchants established in 1947, occupies a rather unusual long building that dates from the 1880's when it was the home of the Conservative Club, later becoming council offices. Just along from here is **Spencer and Ward's** workshop, the last remaining working blacksmith' shop in the town. When Mr Spencer started working here over 70 years ago there were several other blacksmiths' shops in the town with one next door and two down along The Holme. Years ago, horses would literally line up from here down as far as the Crown Hotel waiting to be shod - the rings used for tying up horses can still be seen on the outside wall.

**3.** *At Town Head take the road turning up to the left along the Ingleton Road and follow this road up out of the town passing Gate House then take the turning to the left (Mossy Haw Lane) opposite the entrance to Honeycott Caravan Park. Follow this walled lane down for about half a mile then take the first turning to the left and head down towards Gayle, following the right-hand fork in the road by the small barn. Continue along the lane (Gaits) passing the turning down to the ford, then where the road opens out slightly into a small square head straight on along the cobbled path (Hargill) in front of the cottages to reach the Gayle Bridge.*

**Gate House** was originally a tollhouse on the Lancaster to Richmond turnpike road, when it was known as the Old Toll Bar. During the 19th Century it was the site of the original ropeworks. **Mossy Haw Lane** affords wonderful views of Upper Wensleydale and the surrounding hills that cradle the town - across to the right a narrow strip of tarmac climbs steeply out of Sleddale over Fleet Moss to a height of 589m, the highest road in Yorkshire. A lane known as Gaits turns off down into Gayle, an ancient thoroughfare whose name is derived from the old Norse word 'gata' meaning a street - until the 17th Century Gayle was the main settlement in this area and was more important than neighbouring Hawes.

**4.** *Turn right across Gayle Bridge and follow the road around to the right to reach Gayle Green (now a parking area) beside the ford. Turn left here off the main road along the narrow lane (The Wynd) in between the houses that brings you out again near the bridge. At the bridge turn right along the road (Marridales) to reach a small graveyard on your left. Retrace your steps to the bridge.*

**Gayle Beck,** also known as Duerley Beck, tumbles over a series of rock ledges through the village making an attractive scene. The road that leads round to the right after the bridge is known as Beckstones and boasts a number of lovely old houses including **Clints House,** with its ornate railings and doorway. This house was built by the Routh family in the 18th Century, an important family who are thought to have come to Wensleydale in medieval times and even held posts such as the head Forester of Wensleydale. Note **Yarn House** on the left, a reminder of the days when Gayle was a centre of hand-knitting, a cottage industry that first began in the Dales during the 16th Century as a means for local people to supplement their income. **Gayle Green**

was covered with concrete during the Second World War as a parking area for tanks, and it is still managed by the Trustees of the Manor of Bainbridge. This Manor can be traced back to Norman times, however a group of local people bought the manorial rights in the 17th Century. Perhaps the finest houses in Gayle can be found along Marridales (the Burtersett road) including the **Old Hall** of 1695 as well as **Force Head Farm** that dates from 1711. Next door is the **Gayle Institute** housed in a former Sandemanian Chapel. This religious group was an off-shoot of the Scottish Presbyterian Church, founded in the 18th Century by Robert Sandeman during the period of the Evangelical Revival. Just before the bridge is a lane that leads down to **Gayle Mill,** built in 1784 as a cotton mill although over the years it has also processed wool and wood - Gayle Mill is the oldest unaltered cotton mill in the country. There are plans to restore the mill.

**5.** *Cross Gayle Bridge and head straight on along Gayle Lane back towards Hawes passing the Wensleydale Creamery to reach the road junction by the school.*
The art of making **Wensleydale Cheese** can be traced back to the Cistercian monks who settled in the valley in 1150. Following the Dissolution of the Monasteries, cheese was made on local farms then in 1897 Mr Chapman decided to make cheese on a commercial basis and set up a cheese factory along Gayle Beck in Hawes. Following the difficult years of the 1920's this business faced closure, however, well-known dalesman Kit Calvert MBE rallied enough support from local farmers to save the dairy. The cheese factory moved to its present site along Gayle Lane in 1954, however in 1966 it was bought by the Milk Marketing Board who decided to close it in 1992 and move production to Lancashire! This led to a management buy-out and the thriving business we see today - the only real Wensleydale Cheese in the world. **Hawes Primary School** stands on the corner of the Market Place and Gayle Lane, a fine Victorian school built in 1879 - note the carving of someone milking a cow beneath the small bell turret.

6. *Turn right through the Market Place again keeping to the right-hand side of the road at the bottom of which, where the road divides, continue straight on passing the White Hart Inn. Follow this road winding down, over the old bridge and back to reach the Dales Countryside Museum.*
As you walk back down through the **Market Place,** the area of land on your right that is now occupied by garages, a chip shop and a small car park is known as Penny Garth, where cattle and sheep were penned when the livestock market was held along the main street. The Auction Mart opened in 1887 just outside the town along Burtersett Road, though livestock continued to be sold on the main street until the Great War. The large Market Hall building of 1898, otherwise known as the **Market House,** dominates the Market Place and is still used for markets, meetings and social events. You soon come to the Rock and Gem Shop, a small whitewashed building that used to house **Kit Calvert's Antiquarian Bookshop** until about ten years ago. This

fascinating old bookshop can now be found through the flagged passageway around the corner. Other shops of note include **Elijah Allen & Son,** a traditional family-run grocers that has served the town for over 150 years. The **Church of St Margaret** was built in 1851 and dominates the town's skyline with its soaring tower capped by a distinctive pepper-pot spire. There has been a place of worship at Hawes since at least 1483 when a small chapel was built to serve the travellers through the Forest of Wensleydale and the local inhabitants. A flagged path enclosed by railings leads to the right of the church up to the far graveyard where there is a large stone Celtic Memorial Cross in memory of those who lost their lives when the Express train to Scotland crashed on Christmas Eve 1910 at Hawes Junction killing a dozen passengers. At the foot of the Cross is an inscription to the memory of William Riddell *"Oh! Tell my mother about this will you? She lives in Ayr."* The **White Hart Inn** has changed little since the days when stagecoaches pulled up outside its door en route from Lancaster to Richmond - note the old bell high up on the wall that was once used to summon fresh horses from the stables that occupied the hillside opposite. **Hawes Bridge** lies at the heart of the original settlement of Hawes, a former packhorse bridge that has been modified over the years. From this bridge there is a fine view up along Gayle Beck which cascades over limestone ledges, beside which is **The Old Dairy.** Originally a woollen mill, this building was the home of the Wensleydale Cheese factory before it moved to its present premises along Gayle Lane.

# Helmsley

| | |
|---|---|
| **TIME:** | Two hours |
| **START:** | Feversham Memorial in the centre of the Market Place. |
| **TOILETS:** | Located off Borogate or in the main car park. |
| **CAFÉ:** | Several to choose from; try Nice Things in the Market Place. |
| **PUBS:** | Five pubs to choose from: Black Swan, Feathers, Crown Hotel, Royal Oak and Feversham Arms. |
| **PARKING:** | The Market Place offers limited parking; there is also a large car park off Church Street. |
| **INFORMATION:** | Helmsley Tourist Information Centre: 01439 770173 |
| **MARKET DAY:** | Friday |

> "*Helmsley has served the needs of the people of Ryedale for centuries and still boasts a weekly market, numerous high-quality shops, old coaching inns, Georgian houses and the spectacular ruins of Helmsley Castle.*"

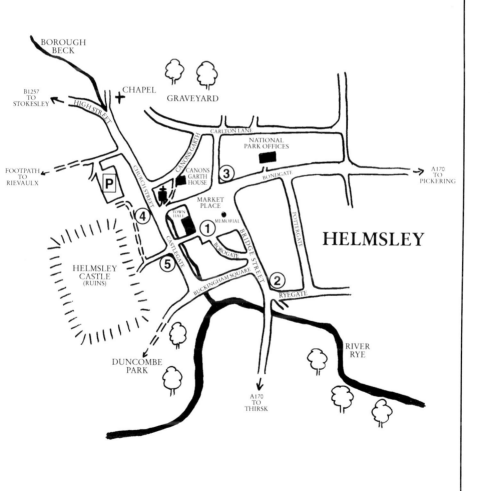

**1.** *From the Feversham Memorial in the centre of the Market Place, head along the main road towards 'Thirsk' (Bridge Street) then as you reach the road bridge across the River Rye take the turning on the left along Ryegate.*

Helmsley is a busy market town on the southern edge of the North York Moors National Park at the point where the deep valley of Ryedale opens out into the flat Vale of Pickering - it is the 'Gateway to the Moors'. It was a Saxon called Helm who first made a clearing in the forest for his small farm around 1,200 years ago and by the time the Normans arrived in the 11th Century there were several families living here in what was known as Elmeslac. The town's development as a bustling market centre began in earnest following the establishment of nearby Rievaulx Abbey in 1132 and the rebuilding of a stronger stone castle. Helmsley has served the needs of the people of Ryedale for centuries and still boasts a weekly market, numerous high-quality shops, old coaching inns, Georgian houses and the spectacular ruins of Helmsley Castle. The first thing that catches your eye as you arrive in Helmsley is the imposing Victorian Gothic canopy over a statue of the Second Lord Feversham (the **Feversham Memorial**), built in 1871 to a design by Sir Gilbert Scott. On the other side of the Market Place is the much older **Market Cross** surrounded by cobbles. Helmsley was granted a weekly Market Charter in 1672, although regular markets had been held here for centuries - the Market Cross used to be situated within the churchyard as in medieval times markets were often held on the Sabbath and within church grounds as many people had to make long journeys to church. The **Market Place** is lined with old coaching inns and fine shops such as Hunter's of Helmsley and Browns department store. Dominating the scene is the **Town Hall,** built in 1901 by Lord Feversham as a court house and market hall. It was given to the town in 1958 and now houses the Tourist Information Centre. Tucked behind the houses through an archway off **Bridge Street** is the old **Friends' Meeting House,** now used as an arts centre, whilst further along the road at No.33 is **Buckingham House,** a superb Georgian house with a fine fan-light window above the door. Just before the road bridge note the narrow gap in the wall that leads down to the river which was once the main source of water for the townsfolk.

**2.** *Walk along Ryegate then take the first turning on the left along Pottergate and follow this up to reach the main road (Bondgate) where you turn left and back into the Market Place.*

**Helmsley Station** once stood at the bottom of Ryegate on the old branch loop between Pickering and the Malton to York line, however a lack of passengers meant that it succumbed to closure in 1953, a full ten years before the Beeching Report. Note the old-fashioned corner shop complete with 'Brooke Bond Tea' and 'Cadbury's' signs in the window. As you turn into **Bondgate** from Pottergate note the row of twelve cottages across the road with their distinctive pitched roofs whilst further along the road to the left is the **Old Vicarage** that now houses the Headquarters of the North York Moors National Park Authority.

**3.** *As you reach the Market Place turn right along the lane between the Crown Hotel and the Black Swan then at the T-junction at the top of this lane turn left and follow the road down to the left. When you reach the Church head through the gate into the churchyard (next to Canons Garth House) and follow the path down passing the main Church entrance to reach the main road again at a road junction.*

During the 18th Century Helmsley developed as an important overnight centre for stagecoaches and once supported several inns and alehouses, many of which have closed over the years. The **Black Swan Hotel** has been welcoming visitors since at least the 18th Century and once boasted a direct stagecoach route to London. This hotel incorporates three distinct buildings with the original inn on the far right, a Georgian house in the middle and a half timbered Tudor house to the left that was once used as the Rectory. The 16th Century **Crown Hotel** has been in the same family for over 40 years and is renowned for its High Yorkshire Tea. Note the old stabling blocks behind the hotels. The tower of **All Saints Church** with its four pinnacles rises above the rooftops, a place of worship since Saxon times although the original stone Norman church was almost completely rebuilt in the 1860's with the exception of the wonderful Norman doorway. Inside are many items of interest including medieval pikes once used by the local constabulary to subdue unruly inhabitants and oak furniture crafted by 'Mousey' Thompson of Kilburn. Before the Dissolution of the Monasteries All Saints' was administered by Augustinian Canons from Kirkham Priory. In 1122 Walter Espec, Lord of Helmsley Castle, established a priory in the Howardian Hills for Augustinian Canons, otherwise known as the 'Black Canons'. A story is told of how Walter Espec's son was out riding one day and was fatally injured when he fell from his horse, and so he erected a stone cross and founded the priory at the scene of the tragedy in memory of his son. Adjacent to the church stands the magnificent half-timbered house known as **Canons Garth** that was originally built by the monks of Kirkham.

**4.** *Turn right along Church Street and follow this up passing the Feversham Arms Hotel and the HSBC Bank (Church Street now becomes High Street) keeping to the right-hand side of the road up to reach the last houses at the top of the street. Cross the road and head back down towards the town along the other side of the road passing Woodard House and the Scout Hut then take the road to the right marked by an old signpost 'Footpath to Rievaulx 3'. Follow this up then where it becomes a rough lane head to the left through the parking area towards the Castle to join a footpath which you follow to the left skirting around the Castle perimeter (signpost 'Market Place') to reach the entrance to the Castle where you turn left down to reach Castlegate.*

**Church Street** is delightful with many attractive cottages, houses and the Feversham Arms Hotel set amongst trees and grassy verges with the diminutive **Borough Beck** flowing through the middle. Just as you are about to leave Helmsley there is a cluster of cottages overlooking a small 'green' with the tiny **Catholic Church of St Mary** hidden away behind the houses. This church was built in 1894 and is served from

Ampleforth Abbey. The imposing stone-built **Woodard House** dates from 1861 and was the town's workhouse for a while. The track that leaves Helmsley near to the parking area is the start of the Cleveland Way, a 110-mile walk from Helmsley to Filey Brigg via the Hambleton and Cleveland Hills as well as the Coast. A fine stone sculpture with a carving of an acorn, the 'National Trail' symbol, marks the start of this walk. Dominating the town are the impressive ruins of **Helmsley Castle,** which date back to 1120 when Walter Espec was given land by Henry I who wanted to strengthen his northern kingdom against the Scots. Only the impressive defensive earthworks remain of this original wooden castle as his brother-in-law Robert de Roos rebuilt the castle in stone in the late 12th Century. Over the centuries the de Roos family grew wealthy through marriage and in 1525 Lord Ros of Helmsley (they lost an 'o' over the centuries) was awarded the Earldom of Rutland due to his support of the Tudor dynasty which later enabled him to purchase the buildings and estates of Rievaulx at a very favourable price following their suppression by Henry VIII. Through marriage the estates passed in the early 17th Century to the Duke of Buckingham, however in 1689 on his death the castle and its estates were bought by Sir Charles Duncombe whose descendants, the Earls of Feversham, still own them. During its heyday the castle was renowned throughout the country for its impregnability due to the many innovative defensive features incorporated into the design including the double earthworks, barbicans and famous D-shaped tower. The castle, however, never saw any action until the English Civil War and was made untenable under Cromwell's orders.

5. *Turn right along Castlegate and follow this round to the left through Buckingham Square to quickly reach Bridge Street again. Turn left along the road then take the lane to the left (Borogate) opposite the Post Office which brings you back into the Market Place.*

**Castlegate** is perhaps the most attractive area of Helmsley with the crystal clear Borough Beck flowing between the road and the old 'crofts' that still run back from the houses that line the Market Place; there is a classic view back along the beck towards the church. Another aspect of Helmsley's development was the production of linen and woollen products that became an important cottage industry, indeed many weavers cottages can still be found in the town and the small bridge behind the Town Hall is known as Dyers Bridge as this was where they used to dye the cloth in the stream. The half-timbered building along Castlegate just after the Yorkshire Bank is known as the **Old Manor House.** This fine house was once an inn where William Wordsworth and his sister stayed in 1802 when they passed through the town on their way to visit William's future bride near Scarborough. The area at the bottom of Castlegate is known as **Buckingham Square** with the entrance to **Duncombe Park** to the right (a fairly long detour!). Duncombe Park was built in 1713 as a replacement for the cold and damp castle, however in 1879 the original 18th Century house was all but destroyed by fire, although the façade was saved and was sympathetically rebuilt

The house is still occupied by Lord Feversham, descendants of the Duncombe family, and is open to the public. The vast formal landscaped gardens are of particular note, a superb example of bold yet romantic 18th Century planned gardens. Where Buckingham Square joins Bridge Street there is a fine 18th Century house on the left that was used as a bank for a while, note the old doorway with the date 1922. The final part of this walk heads up along Borogate, a delightful lane with an array of small shops and businesses including a working blacksmiths and a riding school housed in old stabling blocks that once belonged to a coaching inn.

# Knaresborough

**TIME:** Two & a half hours

**START:** Knaresborough Castle

**TOILETS:** Castle Gardens, Waterside, Conyngham Hall and the Bus Station.

**CAFÉ:** Numerous cafés along Waterside in the shadow of the Castle and Railway Viaduct.

**PUBS:** Several to choose from; try Blind Jack's in the Market Place.

**PARKING:** Parking available in the Castle Gardens or around the Market Place and Gracious Street.

**INFORMATION:** Knaresborough Tourist Information Centre: 01423 866886

**MARKET DAY:** Wednesday

*"Mother Shipton, England's most famous Prophetess, was born in a cave beside the river during a violent storm in 1488. She foretold of the invasion of the Spanish Armada, the Great Fire of London and that 'The World shall end when the High Bridge is thrice fallen' - it has already fallen twice!"*

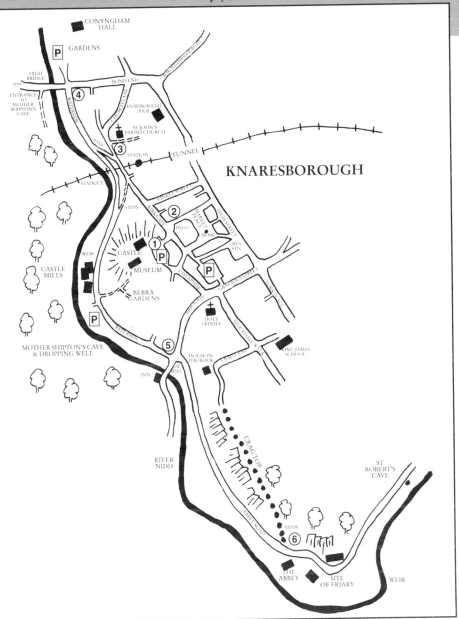

KNARESBOROUGH

*1. From Knaresborough Castle, walk across the parking area passing the Police Station on your right then follow the road bearing round to the left into the Market Place.*

There has been a fortified building on the cliff above the Nidd Gorge since at least Saxon times, however the first castle was built on this site following the Norman Conquest to maintain control over the unruly North. The Castle became a favourite retreat for Royalty who came to hunt in the surrounding Forest of Knaresborough; King John was a frequent visitor. It was completely rebuilt between 1300 and 1312 during Edward I and Edward II's reign when the King's Tower, curtain wall plus many other buildings were built; the castle was once the most impressive in the North with twelve towers rising above the ramparts. For most of its life, **Knaresborough Castle** has been in Royal control or ownership. John of Gaunt, who later became the Duke of Lancaster, was brought up at Knaresborough and following his death in 1399 the Duchy of Lancaster became part of the Crown and it has remained a Royal castle ever since. The Castle's prominence in National and Royal affairs diminished during the 15th and 16th Centuries, however it was during the Civil War in the 1640's that its fate was sealed, as this was a Royalist stronghold at a time when much of Yorkshire supported the Parliamentarians. Following the defeat of the Royalists at the Battle of Marston Moor in 1644, the Castle was ordered to be made untenable by Cromwell. Almost all of the buildings were pulled down except the **Old Courthouse** and the lower floors of the King's Tower, which were used as a prison. The Old Courthouse dates back to the early 14th Century and was in constant use from 1333 until the 19th Century. This Court was responsible for the administration of the Honour of Knaresborough, a vast Royal Estate created after the Norman Conquest divided into Borough (town), Liberty (area north of the River Nidd let as small manors) and the Forest (large hunting forest from the Washburn Valley to the Vale of York). The town of Knaresborough grew as a trading centre in the shadow of the castle. The large **Market Place** still retains much of its character and charm, at the centre of which is a modern **Market Cross** on an 18th Century base; the town was granted a Market Charter in 1310 by Edward II. The **Town Hall** dates from 1862 and replaced a much older Toll Booth; prospective MP's made electioneering speeches from the balcony. The Market Place is also home to **'Ye Oldest Chymist Shoppe in England'**, which opened its doors in 1720 and continued as a chemist shop until 1997; it is now owned by Farrah's, the famous Harrogate Toffee makers. The narrow medieval alleyway to the right of this shop is called **Butter Lane** where dairy products were once sold - the narrow lane and high buildings protected the butter from sunlight.

*2. From the corner of the Market Place near the Town Hall, head down along Kirkgate to reach the Railway Station. Cross the lines (subway) then almost immediately forsake Water Bag Bank for the path that continues straight on to reach St John's Parish Church.*

As you turn into **Kirkgate**, note the row of cottages on your left, which were recorded in 1611 as being a small hospital for six poor folk. Kirkgate quickly leads down to the **Railway Station,** a wonderful example of a Victorian station that dates from the 1840's when a branch line from York was built to connect with the Thirsk to Leeds line at Starbeck. The **Railway Viaduct** dates from 1851 and was designed to complement the Castle with small turrets and battlements. This was the second viaduct to be built as the original one collapsed in 1848 as it neared completion, the fallen masonry caused the river to rise a dozen feet. **Water Bag Bank** leads steeply down to the left and once provided access for the people of the town to collect their water supplies from the river. At the top of the Bank is **Tudor Cottage,** birthplace of Lord Inman of Knaresborough (1892 - 1979), Chairman of Charing Cross Hospital, Chairman of the BBC and Lord Privy Seal. As you walk through the churchyard, note the two-storey house across to the right overlooking the churchyard. This was the home of the **Free Grammar School,** known as King James' School, established on this site in 1616 although the present building dates from 1741; the school moved in 1901. The Parish Church, dedicated to **St John the Baptist,** dates largely from the 13th to 15th Centuries although some stonework from the original Norman structure remains. The Church is noted for its small chapel with many tombs and memorials of the Slingsby family who were large landowners and prominent Royalists. On the floor beside the tomb of Francis and Mary Slingsby is the gravestone of Sir Henry Slingsby who was beheaded in 1658 on Tower Hill following the Civil War. This gravestone is said to have been either the altar stone or even St Robert's gravestone from the Chapel of the Holy Cross at St Robert's Cave. William Slingsby, another member of the family, discovered Tewit Well, which made Harrogate into a world famous Spa Town.

3. *Walk through the churchyard and follow the path / driveway round to the right skirting around the Church along Church Lane (do not walk along The Parsonage). Follow this lane down to reach the main road at Bond End where you turn left down to reach High Bridge.*

**Bond End** is an ancient settlement that originally lay just outside the boundary of the township or 'borough' of Knaresborough. This was where the serfs and peasants, otherwise known as 'bond men', lived. There are many old houses in this area including the half-timbered **St John's House** that dates back to 1498. As you walk down towards High Bridge, note the **Dower House Hotel** on your right, an elegant three storey brick-built house that dates from the 15th Century when it was known as Lylley Hall. Immediately before the bridge on the right are pleasant riverside gardens that lead to **Conyngham Hall,** once the home of Lord Macintosh, the Halifax 'toffee magnate', whose company later became part of Rowntree's of York. A detour across the bridge to the left is the entrance to **Mother Shipton's Cave.** A lovely riverside walk through mature woodland brings you to the Petrifying Well, Wishing Well and Mother Shipton's Cave. The unique Petrifying Well, also known as the Dropping Well, turns everyday items such as teddy bears into stone, a phenomenon that has been attracting visitors since 1630! Mother Shipton, England's most famous

Prophetess, was born in a cave beside the river during a violent storm in 1488. She foretold of the invasion of the Spanish Armada, the Great Fire of London and that "The World shall end when the High Bridge is thrice fallen" - it has already fallen twice!

**4.** *Turn left before High Bridge along Waterside. Follow this all the way down to reach the junction with Briggate at Low Bridge.*
**Waterside** is a pleasant lane that runs alongside the River Nidd with boats for hire, riverside cafés and numerous paths that thread their way up the steep cliffs. You soon come to the foot of Water Bag Bank with **Manor Cottage** on your left, a thatched cottage that is said to be the oldest house in the town, whilst on your right is the **Old Manor House** where King John is reputed to have stayed. The road soon narrows and passes beneath sheer cliffs below the Castle to reach **Castle Mills,** which date from the late 18th Century. Knaresborough was an important centre of linen production particularly from the 16th to 18th centuries, producing some of the finest linen for prestigious clients including the Royal household. Titus Salt was said to have looked at Knaresborough for his mill before settling at a site near Shipley at what became known as Saltaire. Castle Mills stopped producing linen in the 1970's and has since been converted into apartments.

**5.** *At Low Bridge cross the main road and follow Abbey Road directly opposite. Follow this quiet lane for just over half a mile down to reach a large stone-built house on your right called The Abbey. (A short detour straight on will take you to a group of houses and farms where the Trinitarian Friary once stood - St Robert's Cave is a further quarter mile on along the road - return to The Abbey).*

**The House in the Rock** was built during the late 18th Century by Thomas Hill, who lived in the house with his wife and six children! Beside the house is the diminutive **Chapel of Our Lady of the Crag,** a wayside shrine that dates back to 1408 and the third oldest of its kind in the country. **Abbey Road** is a delightful lane set beneath rocky cliffs with many lovely houses leading down to the river. Our route turns up to the left at **The Abbey,** however a short distance further along the road brings you to a group of houses and farms with carved monastic stones set into the walls. This was the site of an important 13th Century **Trinitarian Priory,** a religious order that raised ransom money for Christians held captive during the Crusades. It was controlled by twelve priors when it was dissolved by Henry VIII, following which the lands went to the Slingsby family and the buildings were stripped and left to fall into decay; The Abbey is said to stand on the site of the former gatehouse. **St Robert's Cave** is a further ten-minute walk along Abbey Road. Robert lived a reclusive life in this small cave cut out of the rock with an adjoining chapel from 1180 until his death in 1218. The fame of Robert as a holy man spread throughout the country with many people, including King John, flocking to see him for healing. After his death Robert was buried within this chapel and it quickly became one of main pilgrimage sites in Europe; Robert was made a saint in 1252. The large number of pilgrims was the main reason why the Trinitarians decided to build their priory nearby, indeed in around 1250 St Robert's remains were moved from his chapel to the new Priory.

**6.** *From The Abbey a footpath (signpost) leads steeply up the hillside (steps and railings) to Crag Top. Follow the clear path along Crag Top until you eventually join Crag Lane, which you follow round to the right to reach the main road opposite King James Road. Turn left here along Stockdale Walk and follow this down to Gracious Street, where you turn left then take the first turning to the right along Cheapside. Follow this road down then where it bends round to the right head straight on back to the Castle.*

The large spire of **Holy Trinity Church,** which dates from 1856, dominates the skyline. Cheapside lay on the edge of the ancient town boundary or 'borough', which was marked by a ditch; note the house on the corner dated 1644. As you walk back into the **Castle Gardens,** note the two large sections of wall across to your left. These are all that remain of the large East Gate and barbican built by Edward I, whilst to the left is a well-preserved section of the dry moat. To finish this walk, head over to the King's Tower for the finest view of the town with the river and viaduct far below.

# Leyburn

| | |
|---|---|
| **TIME:** | Two hours |
| **START:** | Leyburn Market Place. |
| **TOILETS:** | Situated along Railway Street and off the Market Place. |
| **CAFÉ:** | Plenty of choice; try The Posthorn in the Market Place or Mrs Pumphrey's along the High Street. |
| **PUBS:** | Five to choose from: the Sandpiper Inn, Golden Lion Hotel, Black Swan Hotel, Bolton Arms and the King's Head |
| **PARKING:** | Large car park just off the Market Place. |
| **INFORMATION:** | Leyburn Tourist Information Centre: 01969 623069 |
| **MARKET DAY:** | Friday |

*"The lane that leads out of the right-hand corner of the Square takes you up onto Leyburn Shawl, a wooded limestone ridge that affords superb views across Wensleydale towards Penhill. According to legend, when Mary, Queen of Scots escaped from Bolton Castle she was recaptured on this ridge after losing her shawl at a spot still known as the Queen's Gap."*

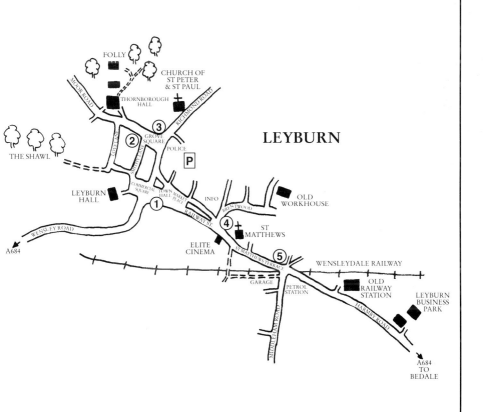

FOLLY

CHURCH OF
ST PETER
& ST PAUL

MOOR ROAD

THORNBOROUGH
HALL

RICHMOND ROAD

GROVE
SQUARE

③

②

THE SHAWL

POLICE

P

**LEYBURN**

LEYBURN
HALL

COMMERCIAL
SQUARE

TOWN
HALL

MARKET
PLACE

INFO

BRENTWOOD

OLD
WORKHOUSE

RAILWAY ST

①

WENSLEY ROAD

A684

ELITE
CINEMA

④

ST
MATTHEWS

ST MATTHEWS TERRACE

⑤

WENSLEYDALE RAILWAY

GARAGE

PETROL
STATION

OLD
RAILWAY
STATION

LEYBURN
BUSINESS
PARK

MIDDLEHAM ROAD

HAWLEY ROAD

A684
TO
BEDALE

**1.** *From the centre of the Market Place walk up passing to the left of the Town Hall, over the main road and into Commercial Square beside the Bolton Arms. Follow the lane out of the right-hand corner of Commercial Square - there are two lanes to choose from, our route heads along the lane to your right (Smithy Lane) down to reach Grove Square.*

Leyburn stands at the gateway to Wensleydale and is a fascinating town with many elegant Georgian and Victorian buildings lining its large Market Place. Leyburn dates from pre-Conquest times, indeed the name of the town is derived from Anglo-Saxon words meaning 'clearing by the stream' - there are several springs and streams in the vicinity. It remained a tiny hamlet until the 16th Century when it began to develop as the trading centre for the lower dale taking over from the once important market town of Wensley that had been devastated by The Plague in 1563. The large **Market Place,** still cobbled in places, is dominated by the imposing **Town Hall.** This rather stark building was completed in 1856, developed by Lord Bolton whose family was instrumental in the growth of Leyburn following the demise of Wensley. The ground floor of the Town Hall has been home to the traditional ironmongers' shop of **Wray Bros.** since around 1918, prior to which the site was occupied by another ironmongers known as Craddocks; Wray Bros have since expanded up onto the first floor! Note the ornate wrought iron **Victorian Drinking Fountain** complete with a lion's head outside the Town Hall, a relic of the first piped fresh water supply into the town. Adjacent to the Town Hall is a **War Memorial** to the local men who gave their lives in the two World Wars. This was where the market cross once stood - Leyburn was granted a Market Charter in 1684 by Charles II. The fine three-storey **Bolton Arms** stands proudly in the corner of Commercial Square, originally built as a shooting lodge for the Duke of Bolton over 200 years ago. **Commercial Square** lies beyond the main Market Place and is lined with a variety of shops and buildings including R. Campbell & Sons, a general store established in 1868; note the old shop sign. An alley leads down between the old two-storey cottages on the corner of Commercial Square and the High Street to the **Beech End Model Village,** a 'hands on' model village complete with working trains, cars and boats. Set into the wall of this alleyway is an ancient water pump, originally used to pump water out of the cellars of the surrounding houses. In the far left-hand corner of the Square are the gates to **Leyburn Hall** (private), a large Georgian house almost hidden by trees that was once the home of the Yarker family, an old and well-known Dales family. The lane that leads out of the right-hand corner of the Square takes you up onto **Leyburn Shawl,** a wooded limestone ridge that affords superb views across Wensleydale towards Penhill. According to legend, when Mary, Queen of Scots escaped from Bolton Castle she was recaptured on this ridge after losing her shawl at a spot still known as the Queen's Gap. A more likely explanation for the name comes from the Old Scandinavian word 'schall' meaning a group of huts, as this was probably the site of the original settlement.

**2.** *At Grove Square, turn left along Moor Road heading out of the town to quickly reach Thornborough House on your right. From here retrace your steps back into Grove Square along the left-hand side of the road down to reach the junction with the High Street / Richmond Road.*

**Grove Square** was Leyburn's original market place but as the town developed a larger market square was required so in 1800 the present Market Place was laid out. During the 18th and 19th Centuries Leyburn grew prosperous as a trading centre for livestock, farm produce and wool - many of the town's finest buildings date from this period. **Secret Garden House** on your left is a substantial Georgian property surrounded by mature gardens, said to have been the dower house for the widows of Grove Hall and also where Peter Goldsmith lived, Lord Nelson's surgeon. To the rear of the house at the top of **Love Lane** is a small building that housed the New Theatre from 1794 until 1865. The large house on the right along Moor Road is **Thornborough Hall**, originally known as Grove Hall. Ownership of the house passed to the Thornburgh family in the early 18th Century, a family of some distinction from Westmorland, hence the change of name. In the late 18th Century the house again changed hands, this time to the wealthy Riddell family who laid out the formal gardens in the early 19th Century - look out for the Georgian 'Gothic' style folly hidden in the trees. The present Thornborough Hall was built in 1863 under the guidance of Francis Riddell and replaced the earlier Georgian hall. This 'new' Victorian hall was reputedly designed by York architect Joseph Hansom, more famous for his 'Hansom Cab'; the building now houses the town library. As you walk back down through **Grove Square** you pass a number of attractive houses including Grove Hotel with its datestone of 1757, then two houses set back from the road above which towers a monkey puzzle tree and finally a row of old cottages, built in characteristic Dales' style.

3. *At the bottom of Grove Square turn right along the High Street then turn left immediately before the Town Hall. Walk down the left-hand side of the Market Place, at the bottom of which continue straight on along the lane passing the Methodist Church on your left to reach a road junction at the Sandpiper Inn. A short detour to the left along Brentwood takes you to Quarry Hills (Victorian Workhouse). Retrace your steps back to the main road (Railway Street).*

A short detour to the left along Richmond Road at the bottom of Grove Square quickly brings you to the **Roman Catholic Church of St Peter and St Paul,** which was built in 1835 on land given by Francis Riddell of Thornborough Hall. This is one of the earliest Catholic churches in the country built following centuries of suppression of the 'Old Faith'; the spacious interior with its box pews has altered little in the intervening years. As you walk back into Grove Square you pass a wonderful example of a Victorian **Police Station,** built in 1877 complete with an archway for horse-drawn carriages. Further along the High Street on your left is a shop with the initials 'WLA' and 1746 inscribed above the doorway. This was the birthplace in 1766 of **Francis L'Anson,** Leyburn's most famous daughter, who later moved to London and married Leonard McNally who immortalised her in the song "The Sweet Lass of Richmond Hill"; the initials above the door are of her father William L'Anson. On the opposite side of the road are a number of interesting shops and buildings including the **HSBC Bank,** housed in an ornate Victorian building that was originally a branch of the Darlington District Joint Stock Banking Company. The **Market Place** still retains many elegant buildings, some with their original frontages such as the **Black Swan Hotel,** a fine three-storey inn complete with a large mantrap attached to the outside wall. Numerous lanes lead from the Market Place behind these old inns to where there was once stabling, outbuildings and yards. As you head out of the bottom corner of the Market Place you pass the **Methodist Church** on your left, built in the 1880's with a particularly fine Rose Window. Situated a short distance along Brentwood is a fine example of a **Victorian Workhouse** built in 1877. This wonderful stone building has since been converted into private flats known as Quarry

Hills, although back in the 19th Century only the poorest people of the Parish would have sought refuge at such a formidable institution.

**4.** *Turn left along the main road passing St Matthews Church on your left and head straight on along St Matthews Terrace to reach the bridge across the railway lines at the junction with Middleham Road. Continue straight on along Harmby Road to reach the old Railway Station on your left. Retrace your steps back up to reach the railway bridge at the junction with Middleham Road.*

For centuries Leyburn did not have its own Parish Church but was served by the ancient Holy Trinity Church at Wensley, however, in 1868 **St Matthews Church** was built to serve the needs of the burgeoning population. As you walk out of the town along **St Matthews Terrace** you pass a row of large Victorian villas built following the arrival of the railway. Work began on the **Wensleydale Railway** in 1848 to connect the main line at Northallerton with the Settle to Carlisle Railway at Garsdale, although it took a full thirty years to complete the line in its entirety - the railway reached Leyburn in 1856. The railway closed for passenger services in 1954, although the tracks were kept between Northallerton and Redmire to service the limestone quarries and, more recently, to transport M.o.D. equipment to the ranges above Wensleydale. The Wensleydale Railway Association was formed in 1990 to try to re-establish the link to Garsdale and resume passenger services along the existing track - services look set to resume as far as Leyburn with plans to extend the line to Aysgarth and beyond. The old **Railway Station** forms an integral part of the efforts to re-open the line; here you will find the Wensleydale Railway Shop housed in the old waiting rooms. A five minute walk along Harmby Road out of the town will take you to the **Leyburn Business Park,** where you will find the Violin Making Workshop as well as the Leyburn Teapottery famed for their rather unusual hand-made teapots. Further along the road is the large purpose-built auction house of Tennants Auctioneers, one of the most famous auction houses outside London.

**5.** *At the junction on the railway bridge take the track ahead of you off Middleham Road immediately to the right of the garage workshop (R & S Motors) heading up with the railway tracks down to your right. This track soon divides, follow the right-hand branch that heads over a railway bridge and up to join the main road opposite the Church. Turn left back up into the Market Place.*

The **Elite Cinema** opened in 1930 and is a rare survivor of the golden age of the 'silver screen', its small auditorium only seats 170 people. The cinema closed during the 1960's although it remained as a small theatre for the local Amateur Dramatics Society, however in 1994 the Elite reopened once again as a cinema.

# Malton

| | |
|---|---|
| **TIME:** | Two & a half hours |
| **START:** | St Michael's Church, Market Place. |
| **TOILETS:** | Situated in the Market Place |
| **CAFÉ:** | Several to choose from: try Murray's Coffee House in the Market Place or the Yorkshire Tea Rooms along Castlegate. |
| **PUBS:** | Plenty of choice: try the King's Head, Green Man, Golden Lion or the Royal Oak in the Market Place, Suddaby's Crown Hotel in Wheelgate or the Royal Oak and the Wentworth Arms in Old Malton. |
| **PARKING:** | Parking available around the Market Place or off Newbiggin. |
| **INFORMATION:** | Malton Tourist Information Centre: 01653 600048 |
| **MARKET DAY:** | Saturday |

> *"The ownership of the Manor House then passed to his two daughters who could not agree over how to share their inheritance and so in 1674 it was demolished and the stones divided between them - only this gatehouse was left standing!"*

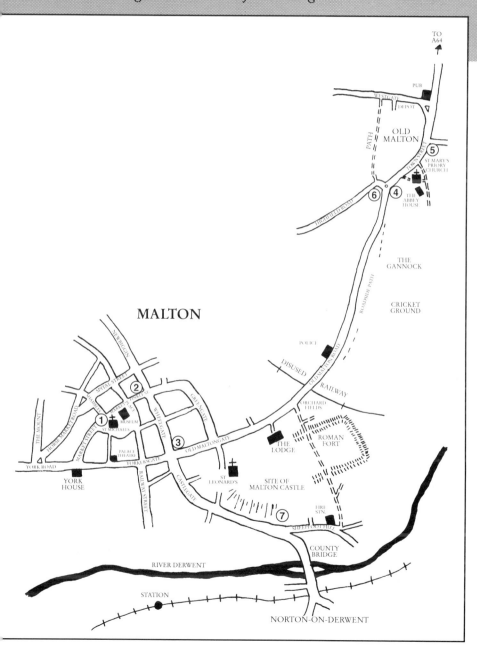

**1.** *From the open Market Place in front of St Michael's Church, walk up through the Market Place passing to the left of the Church to reach the Malton Museum, where you continue straight on down along Finkle Street to reach Wheelgate.*

Malton's **Market Place** is delightful with many hidden corners lined by a variety of old-fashioned shops and inns, as well as a particularly narrow alleyway just to the side of the church. The **Parish Church of St Michael** stands proudly in the middle of this Market Place, established in Norman times, probably to serve the fledgling community that had developed around the castle. In the 12th Century it was given to the Gilbertine Canons of St Mary's Priory at Old Malton as a Chapel-of-Ease. The church was heavily restored in the 19th Century, though some Norman stonework remains in the North and South Aisles. The west (upper) side of the Market Place boasts many old buildings including The Green Man, an ancient coaching inn with a large stone inglenook fireplace, and the ivy-clad Kings Head with its distinctive double pitched roof and coaching arch. You soon come to the turning up along **The Shambles** with its many small individual shops that were once home to the towns' butchers' shops; 'shambles' is derived from the old word for 'meat stall'. This lane leads up to the **Cattle Market,** where livestock are traded in open pens on the street - Malton has been an important trading centre for almost 2,000 years. Our route continues through the Market Place, passing the shop of 'G. Woodall & Son Ltd. Rope, Net and Cover makers' with its lovely façade, to reach the **Malton Museum**. This imposing building was built in the 18th Century as the Butter Market and was later used as the Town Hall before becoming a museum in 1982; you can still see the stone arches of the old market hall inside. Electioneering speeches were once made from the balcony at the front of this building - Malton's most famous MP was Edmund Burke from 1780 until 1794, the noted British statesman and political philosopher. Malton Museum houses one of the most important collections of Roman artefacts in the North, much of which was unearthed at Orchard Fields, the site of Malton's Roman Fort.

**2.** *Turn right down Wheelgate passing the Cross Keys pub then take the first turning on the right along St Michael Street. This quickly leads up into a corner of the Market Place again, where you turn left along Saville Street to reach Yorkersgate. Turn left and follow this main road until you come to the traffic lights at the road junction with Castlegate and Wheelgate.*

Beneath **The Cross Keys** is a relic of medieval Malton, for the cellar of this pub is actually a stone-vaulted crypt, one of three hospices built by the Canons of St Mary's Priory where pilgrims and travellers were offered shelter for the night; no trace remains of the other two. It is reputed that a secret passage links this crypt with St Mary's Priory. **Saville Street** leads down from the Market Place, along which is a large cream-coloured building with columns and scrolls that now houses a carpet shop but was originally built as the **Ebenezer Congregational Church** in 1812. Down from here is the fine **Wesleyan Chapel** of 1811 with its lovely stained glass windows. From the main crossroads along Yorkersgate, a short detour to the left along Wheelgate brings you to **Suddaby's Crown Hotel,** which has been run by five generations of the Suddaby family. Situated in the old stable block behind this former coaching inn is the **Malton Brewery Company,** which was established in 1985 and now supplies around 20 outlets with its well-known beers including Double Chance Bitter, named after a 1920's Grand National winner that had been stabled where the brewery is now. This area, particularly Norton-on-Derwent across the river, has a long tradition of racehorse training.

**3.** *At the crossroads continue straight on, heading up along Old Maltongate. Follow this road up passing The Lodge on your right and then Orchard Fields (Roman Fort) and carry on for a further half a mile to reach a mini-roundabout on the outskirts of Old Malton.*

As you walk along **Old Maltongate,** a short detour to the right along Church Hill brings you to **St Leonard's Church** with its distinctive tower that dominates the town's skyline. This church was founded in the 12th Century as another Chapel-of-Ease for St Mary's Priory and was probably built to serve the neighbouring castle. St Leonard's was returned to the Catholic Church as a gesture of goodwill in 1971, some

400 years after the Reformation. Hidden behind a high stone wall is the **Old Lodge Hotel,** a magnificent building of mellow stone that was built on the site of Malton Castle for Lord Eure in 1602 as the gatehouse of his **Jacobean Manor House.** During the Civil War, Lord Eure sided with the Royalists and was subsequently killed at the Battle of Marston Moor. The ownership of the Manor House then passed to his two daughters who could not agree over how to share their inheritance and so in 1674 it was demolished and the stones divided between them - only this gatehouse was left standing! **Malton Castle** was built in the 11th Century by the de Vesci family over the remains of the Roman Fort. Around a century later the castle passed to Eustace Fitz-John who rebuilt it in stone and gave land in 'old' Malton to the Gilbertine Order for their Priory and also founded the 'borough' of Malton, the 'new' Malton of today. The castle played an important role during the conflicts with Scotland in the 12th and 13th Centuries with the Scots taking control of the castle and surrounding area for a while, indeed in 1322 Robert Bruce captured and destroyed it. It was during this period of unrest that the town walls were built with four gates, or bars, that defined the boundaries of 'new' Malton - Yorkersgate, Wheelgate, Old Maltongate and Castlegate. The Eure family became Lords of the Manor of Malton (and inherited the castle) in the 14th Century and then in about 1600 they cleared away the ruins of the old castle to make way for their new Manor House. Our route now follows Old Maltongate passing Orchard Fields (see Section 6) and the town's cricket and rugby fields all the way to reach Old Malton.

**4.** *At the mini-roundabout follow Town Street (the main road slightly to your right) and follow this down to reach St Mary's Priory Church. Walk through the churchyard passing to the right of the Church, through a stone archway that leads onto a track by the entrance to Abbey House. Turn left here down to the main road again.*

**Old Malton** is quite separate from the town of Malton, or 'new' Malton, having its own character with lovely stone cottages and farmhouses lining the winding main street. This was the site of the original settlement of Malton founded by Anglo-Saxon farmers in around the 7th Century away from the ruins of the abandoned Roman Fort. Remains of an Anglo-Saxon cross have been found near St Mary's Priory Church and it is thought that this may have been an important settlement within the ancient Kingdom of Northumbria visited by Saxon kings. This settlement developed further in Norman times as it lay alongside the Gilbertine Priory, however it gradually diminished in favour of the new town beside the Norman castle. We soon reach **St Mary's Priory Church** with its incredible West Doorway and large tower. The Priory was founded in 1150 by Eustace Fitz-John for Gilbertine Canons, the only native British Monastic Order that had been established in 1131 by St. Gilbert of Sempringham in Lincolnshire; by the time of its suppression by Henry VIII there were twenty-six Gilbertine houses throughout the country. This Church is the finest surviving example of a Gilbertine Priory and the only one still in use for worship in the world. Following the Dissolution the buildings fell into disrepair, so much so that in 1636 the Central Tower was taken down and then in 1732 the Church was reduced in size much to its present form. In its heyday this would have been a magnificent Priory almost treble its present size with double towers soaring above the West Doorway and a large Central Tower above the nave, aisles, transepts and chancel. There were also associated buildings including a refectory, dormitory, guesthouse, infirmary and brewhouse; the evidence of this large monastic site can be seen all around the Church. The Priory Church of today boasts some magnificent Norman, Early English and Perpendicular stonework and houses a wealth of treasures. Behind it is a fine Norman archway that once led into the Cloisters. The Abbey, also known as **Abbey House,** was built probably during the 18th Century using the stones of the ruined Priory and stands on the site of the refectory and cloisters. Beneath one of its outbuildings is a vaulted Undercroft, the only sizeable remains of the living quarters of the Priory. Charles Dickens stayed at Abbey House when it belonged to his friend Charles Smithson, who is buried in the churchyard; the house is now a private residential home.

**5.** *At the main road turn right (Town Street) and follow this down until the road opens out with the Wentworth Arms across to your left. Turn left here along Westgate by the side of the pub and follow this lane down passing the North Yorkshire County Council Depot and West Fold then just before the last houses on your left (where the road becomes a rougher lane) take the footpath to the left. Follow this clear path all the way down to reach Highfield Road where you turn left to quickly reach the mini-roundabout again on the Old Malton Road.*

Town Street once formed part of the main road from York to Scarborough; note the old North Riding of Yorkshire milepost complete with distances to Pickering, Whitby, Malton and York. The road soon opens out into a small 'green' area overlooked by the **Old School House** on the right, with its attractive bell tower, clock and weather vane. Just on from here is an old weighbridge set into the road made by Samuel Dennison & Son of Leeds in 1887, another example of how important this trade route once was. The attractive ivy-covered **Wentworth Arms** is named after Sir Thomas Wentworth who acquired the Manor of Old and New Malton in 1712, from whom it passed to Earl Fitzwilliam. **Westgate** is a lovely quiet lane of some considerable age - 'gata' is the Scandinavian word for street - and still has some thatched cottages.

**6.** *Turn right along the Old Malton Road back to reach Orchard Fields (a pleasant path runs parallel to the main road on the left). At Orchard Fields turn left along the footpath immediately before the row of stone cottages and follow the clear path straight on with the earthworks of the Roman Fort to your left. The path leads down to the bottom right-hand corner of the field out onto Sheepfoot Hill by the Fire Station. Turn right to reach Castlegate.*

The ramparts and earthworks of the **Derventio Roman Fort** can be clearly seen around **Orchard Fields,** with a number of interpretative boards that help bring the area to life. In around AD69 the kingdom of the native British tribes of the North - the Brigantes - collapsed and the Roman Sixth Legion marched north of the Humber to take control of their land. York became the Roman Military Headquarters and forts were built throughout the North to stamp their authority on the area. When the Romans arrived at Malton they were expecting fierce opposition from the Brigantes, however the eastern area of Yorkshire was controlled by the Parisi tribe, a more peaceful tribe who originated from the Seine Valley in France. The Romans originally built a huge fort at Malton in AD71, known as Derventio, that could accommodate 30,000 troops and covered thirty acres - Housesteads Fort along Hadrian's Wall was only around five acres. The Fort was built to defend the important river crossing at the eastern end of the Kirkham Gap between the Howardian Hills and the Yorkshire Wolds and so protect the trade routes between the Vales of York and Pickering. However, with little military threat, this was soon replaced by a smaller fort of around eight acres, manned by an auxiliary regiment. The Fort was rebuilt in stone early in the 2nd Century and was continually garrisoned until the end of Roman occupation in AD410, albeit with varying levels of troops depending on how the northern tribes were behaving! A large civilian settlement grew to the south of this Fort known as the **Vicus** with industries such as metal, jet and bone workshops, bakeries, pottery kilns and even a goldsmith that served the Roman garrison as well as the many traders it attracted. This area became an important trading centre for agriculture from the fertile Vale of Pickering, as it still is today. Excavations have revealed around twenty houses, some showing signs of great wealth with superb mosaic floors; it is thought that there are many more waiting to be discovered.

*7. Head right along Castlegate and follow this road up to reach the crossroads again at the junction with Wheelgate. Turn left here and head up Yorkersgate then take the turning to the right along Market Street opposite York House back into the Market Place.*

**Malton Bridge,** otherwise known as the County Bridge as it once separated the old North and East Ridings of Yorkshire, spans the River Derwent with Norton-on-Derwent on the other side of the riverbank. The present stone bridge dates from the 18th Century, however there has been a river crossing here for 2,000 years. The River Derwent is prone to flooding as it drains much of the North York Moors. In November 2000 this whole area was hit by some of the worst flooding ever with the railway lines and surrounding properties under several feet of water. The **River Derwent** was made navigable between Malton and the River Ouse to the north of Goole during the early 18th Century and for many years was a busy waterway until the arrival of the railways in the mid 19th Century. **Castlegate** lies on the line of a Roman Road - there were several in this area radiating from the Fort. Malton was once a famous brewing centre with two well-known breweries along Castlegate.

**Russell and Wrangham's** was bought by Cameron's in the 1961 and subsequently closed. The old brewery buildings were demolished in the 1980's to make way for a new supermarket. Near the top of Castlegate are the old buildings of the **Charles Rose Brewery,** now flats and offices known as The Maltings. This brewery's heritage stretched back to 1767 but was acquired by Tetley's of Leeds in 1965 and closed in 1969. As you walk up along Yorkersgate, note the large **Palace Theatre** building, built in 1845 by Earl Fitzwilliam as the Corn Exchange, however it was never used as such and later became a cinema. **Chancery Lane** leads up to the side of this building, along which is a brick-built Georgian house that provided Charles Dickens with the inspiration for Scrooge's office in 'A Christmas Carol' - Dickens was a regular visitor to the town. Just up from the Palace Theatre is the imposing 'Subscription Rooms Anno 1814', a stark building that originally housed the **Malton Literary Institute Subscription Rooms** as well as a small theatre. Opposite the turning along Market Street is **York House,** a fine 17th Century house that stands on the site of the Yorkersgate Bar, or gate, into the medieval walled town. Further along Yorkersgate is the **Talbot Hotel,** an elegant three-storey old coaching inn that dates from the late 17th Century when it was built as a mansion house. It became the first hotel in the area during the 18th Century and attracted wealthy people who stayed here on their way to the coastal Spa of Scarborough.

# Masham

| | |
|---|---|
| **TIME:** | One & a half hours |
| **START:** | Masham Market Place |
| **TOILETS:** | Just off Little Market Place |
| **CAFÉ:** | Several to choose from in the Town Centre; try Bordar House in the Market Place. |
| **PUBS:** | Four to choose from: the White Bear, Bay Horse, Bruce Arms and the King's Head. |
| **PARKING:** | In the main Market Place. |
| **INFORMATION:** | Leyburn Tourist Information: 01969 623069 |
| **MARKET DAYS:** | Wednesday and Saturday |

> *"Masham, pronounced 'Massum' if you want to sound like a local, is an attractive grey-stone market town set in the lower reaches of Wensleydale. It is famed for its large Market Place lined with 18th Century houses, historic annual Sheep Fair and two breweries."*

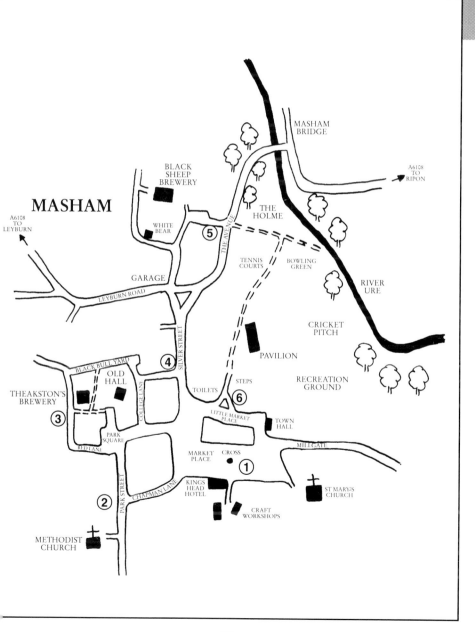

MASHAM

*1. From the Market Cross (facing the King's Head) head across the main Market Place diagonally to the right then follow Chapman Lane out of the corner of the Market Place and on to reach Park Street.*

Masham, pronounced 'Massum' if you want to sound like a local, is an attractive grey-stone market town set in the lower reaches of Wensleydale. It is famed for its large Market Place lined with 18th Century houses, historic annual Sheep Fair and two breweries. Masham has been an important market town since it was granted its market charter in 1393 by Richard II - weekly markets are still held as they have been for six centuries. Masham's **Market Place,** one of the largest in the North of England, is lined with elegant 17th and 18th Century houses, still cobbled around the old tree-shaded market cross. Of particular note is the imposing three-storey **Kings Head Hotel,** a fine stone-built Georgian coaching inn with a wonderful façade. Through the archway to the side of this hotel are the old stabling blocks and outbuildings, now home to a variety of craft workshops where you can watch handthrown pottery being made at **Masham Pottery** or glassblowing at **Uredale Glass.** The monks of Fountains and Jervaulx Abbeys had grazing lands in this area and the town grew in importance as the main sheep market for the Dales. This survives today as the **September Sheep Fair,** which at its height in the 19th Century saw over 70,000 sheep changing hands. **Chapman Lane** leads out of the Market Place, once the main route out of town westwards over the moors to Wharfedale; 'chapman' is the old name for a travelling pedlar. On the corner of Chapman Lane and Park Street are a row of small **almshouses.** A plaque proclaims that Anne Danby and Vernon Harcourt built them in AD1853 "in humble gratitude to God for all his mercies and blessings." As you emerge on Park Street across to your left is the imposing **Methodist Church** set back from the road behind attractive gardens.

*2. Turn right along Park Street then where the road turns sharply right at the HSBC bank head straight on passing to the left of the bank. At the gates to Park House turn left along a footpath and follow this all the way down to reach Red Lane.*
Park Street is an interesting mixture of small cottages as well as Georgian and Victorian houses, overlooked by the HSBC Bank that is housed in the former **Mechanics Institute,** built in 1856. These Institutes were built throughout the country during the 19th Century to provide free education for the working classes and, hopefully, improve their lives; the Mechanics Institute was founded by Mr Birkbeck of Settle - a Yorkshireman! **Park House** can be glimpsed through its gates set amongst mature trees. It reputedly stands on the site of an early medieval Manor House, adjacent to which is the brewery of **T & R Theakston Ltd** that dates back to 1827, famed for its 'Old Peculier' Yorkshire ale. This classic stone-built Victorian brewery became part of Scottish and Newcastle Breweries, as it was then known, in 1987. There is a fascinating Visitor Centre, known as the Black Bull in Paradise, as well as a working cooper's shop where one of the remaining eight brewery coopers in the country is employed making wooden casks for local beer deliveries. Once a small

country brewer with a handful of pubs, Theakston's ales are now available throughout the country - to cope with demand much of the production now takes place at Scottish Courage's Newcastle-upon-Tyne Brewery.

**3.** *Turn right along Red Lane passing Theakston's Brewery on your right then where the road bends round to the left take the lane to the right immediately after the brewery buildings. Follow this lane down passing the entrance to Theakston's Brewery Visitor Centre and on towards the 'Market Square' following it round to the right at the houses then left along College Lane to reach Silver Street.*

Just as you turn left down to reach Silver Street, take a short detour to the right along **College Lane.** The imposing stone and brick house ahead of you is **College House,** an ancient building that has been modified over the years. This was where the 'Peculier Court of the Prebend of Masham' met prior to Henry VIII's Dissolution of the Monasteries. This ecclesiastical Court can trace its origins back to the 12th Century when the Parish of St Mary was given to York Minster who then formed a Prebend and Canonry. The Court had jurisdiction over the local inhabitants with regard to 'particular' offences such as not attending church, swearing, drunkenness and fortune-telling - 'peculier' means 'particular' in Norman-French. College House has been extensively rebuilt over the intervening centuries.

**4.** *Turn left along Silver Street, bearing left at the fork in the road down to reach the main road opposite a garage where you cross over along the road opposite. Follow this road down towards Black Sheep Brewery then where the road bends round to the left at the houses head down along the lane to the right.*

**Silver Street** is home to a number of quality family-run shops including Beaver's Butchers which is renowned for its award-winning sausages ('Beavers the name, for sausages, meat and game'), Reah's Delicatessen Shop that sells just about everything and a general hardware shop. The 'original' **White Bear** pub once stood on the area of open ground to the right of the garage. On the 16th April 1941 a parachute mine was dropped by an enemy plane and landed on the pub killing four local people and two soldiers - the pub was rebuilt further back from the road. The large complex of stone buildings ahead of you was originally **Lightfoot's Brewery** which was taken over by Theakston's back in 1919 - the offices of Theakston's as well as the 'new' White Bear are still housed in some of the old brewery buildings. Following a takeover by Scottish and Newcastle Breweries of his family firm in 1987, Paul Theakston set up the **Black Sheep Brewery** in the old Lightfoot's brewery maltings literally next door to the offices of his old family company. Black Sheep Brewery produces a range of traditional Yorkshire ales using only the finest ingredients and traditional brewing plant rescued from Hartley's of Ulverston. The pronounced bitterness and characteristic flavour of the beers is reminiscent of the old West Riding brews due to the fact that traditional Yorkshire Stone Square fermenting vessels are used. There is an excellent Visitor Centre offering brewery tours, shop, bistro and bar.

**5.** *Follow this lane round to the right down to reach the main road again (The Avenue). Cross the road and take the rough track opposite that leads down across The Holme, turning sharp right at the small parking area and up passing between the tennis courts and bowling green to reach the cricket pavilion. Head up the steps behind the Pavilion that lead back up into the Little Market Place adjacent to the Bruce Arms pub.*

As you emerge onto The Avenue look over to your right across the wide road junction to see the ornate **Fountain** built in 1887 to commemorate Queen Victoria's Golden Jubilee. **Masham Bridge** is a graceful stone structure dating from 1754 which now carries motorists over the River Ure on their way up into Wensleydale. The avenue of mature trees that line the road down to the bridge (hence the name of The Avenue) were planted to commemorate the opening of the branch railway in 1875 from the Ripon to Northallerton line. **Masham Station** was situated across the river away from the town, which probably explains why the line closed to passengers in 1930, a full 30 years before the Beeching Axe closed virtually all of the country's other branch lines. The area of parkland between the tree-lined road and the river is known as **The Holme,** a favourite place for people to walk their dogs or take a Sunday stroll. The **Recreation Ground** with its cricket pitch, tennis courts and bowling green was given to the town by Lord Masham as a memorial to the local men who fought in the Great War.

**6.** *Turn left through the Little Market Place and follow the road round to the right at the Town Hall back into the main Market Place.*

Note the old stone-built **Police House** dated 1891, which is still in (very occasional) use. The **Town Hall** dates from 1913 but was used only a few years later as a convalescent home for soldiers during the First World War; infantry from Leeds were stationed nearby at Breary Banks in Colsterdale. The lane that leads off the Market Place is called **Millgate** and leads down to a 17th Century mill - this was the main road into Masham Centuries ago by way of a ford across the River Ure before the stone bridge was built further upstream. On the left along Millgate is the **Old Grammar School** that was founded in 1760 by William Danby, Lord of the Manor and owner of the Swinton Estate whose widow rebuilt the school in 1834; it is still used as a school. Further along Millgate on the left is the **Old Poor House. St Mary's Church** was founded in Anglo-Saxon times and has a rare example of a 9th Century **Anglo-Saxon Cross** opposite the front door with weather-worn carvings depicting animals as well as people which are thought to represent Our Lord and the Twelve Disciples. Much of the present church dates from the 14th and 15th Centuries, although there is some Norman stonework at the base of the tower, which is crowned by a tall 15th Century spire. For centuries this church had close connections with York Minster as it was given to York in the 12th Century to form a Prebend and Canonry, an important and wealthy Parish which was also given its own ecclesiastical court - the 'Peculier Court of the Prebend of Masham'. This came to an end following the Dissolution of the Monasteries when the powers of the court were transferred to Trinity College, Cambridge who still retain associations until this day. The 'Seal of the Official of the Peculier of Masham 1741' is used as the company logo of Theakston's, who also named their strong ale after this 'Peculier' Court.

# Middleham

**TIME:** One & a half hours

**START:** Market Cross in the main Market Place.

**TOILETS:** Through the passageway to the side of the Richard III Hotel.

**CAFÉ:** Several to choose from including Durants Tea Rooms, The Nosebag Tea Shop and Castle Tea Rooms.

**PUBS:** Try either the White Swan, Black Bull, Richard III Hotel or the Black Swan Hotel.

**PARKING:** On-street parking in either the Market Place or near the Swine Cross.

**INFORMATION:** Leyburn Tourist Information Centre: 01969 623069

> *"Richard Neville, the Earl of Warwick (The Kingmaker),
> inherited the castle in 1461, which brought it firmly into the
> spotlight of National events, especially during the War of the Roses.
> Richard Plantaganet, later Richard III, grew up at the castle
> where he later met his wife Lady Anne Neville, the daughter
> of the Earl of Warwick."*

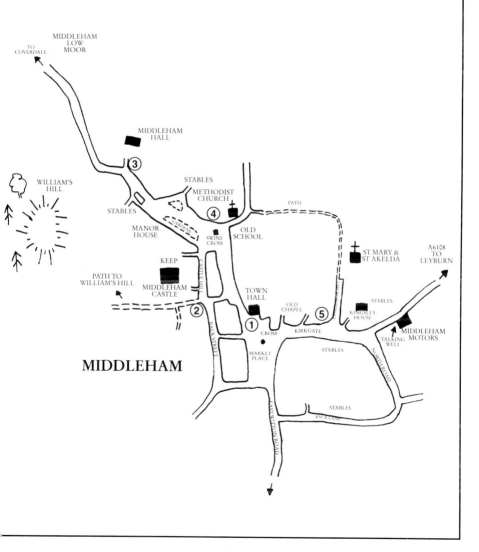

MIDDLEHAM

**1.** *From Market Cross, head up along the road that leaves the top of the Market Place (signed 'Middleham Castle'). Where the road opens out after the Central Stores on your right, turn left across the cobbles and follow the lane up to reach the Castle.* Middleham means 'middle farmstead' and was first settled by Anglo-Saxon farmers in the 7th Century, however it was in the years following the Norman Conquest that the first wooden castle was built on a ridge to the south of the present castle; it was this that provided the stimulus for the growth of Middleham as a town. The focal point of the gently sloping cobbled **Market Place** is the ancient **Market Cross**, crowned by a small cross - a reminder to traders to deal fairly. The town was granted a Market Charter back in 1388 by Richard II, although the weekly markets are no longer held. The Market Place is lined with a wonderful array of Georgian houses and inns with one or two older cottages sandwiched in between, all of which combines to give the town a lovely time-mellowed atmosphere. Buildings of note include **Durants,** originally the Wensleydale Temperance Hotel as the fading painted sign on the gable end testifies. The **White Swan Hotel** is a fine Georgian inn, although it was severely damaged by fire recently and had to be extensively rebuilt. At the bottom of the Market Place is **Jasmine House**, a well-proportioned Georgian house. The two small cottages to the left of the 17th Century **Black Swan Hotel** have survived the rebuilding 'phase' during the 18th Century - the cottage with the date '1682' was once the Golden Lion Inn. **'Domus'** stands at the top of the Market Place, an ivy-clad Georgian house which, unusually, is built of bricks as the wealthy owners wanted to differentiate themselves from the other homeowners in the town who had plundered stones from the castle. The ground floor shop, still with its 19th Century frontage, was originally a plumbers and ironmongers. The building on the corner at the top of the Market Place is **Middleham Town Hall**, built in 1862 and now used as a community centre and home of the Town Council; note the small Stable Lads Welfare Trust shop next door, a reminder of the importance of racing in Middleham. The road quickly opens out as you head towards the smaller Swine Market. On your right is **Glasgow House,** built by Lord Glasgow in 1800 whose stables famously trained the first four home in the St Leger in 1822; it is still used as a stables.

**2.** *Turn right in front of the Castle along Castle Hill then, as the lane begins to open out into the Swine Market, take the lane to the left after Castle Cottage and walk up with the gardens on your right and old cottages on your left. Follow this cobbled lane up between the houses until you come to the main road on the edge of the town with the ornate gates of Middleham Hall across the road to your right.*
Following the Norman Conquest, William the Conqueror gave Alan the Red of Brittany land in what is now North Yorkshire to subdue the unruly North. He built a massive stone fortress at Richmond and a wooden motte and bailey castle at Middleham on the ridge of land to the south of the present castle. The impressive earthworks of this early Norman castle, known as **William's Hill,** can still be seen. Legend says that if you run round this hill seven times then an entrance will open to

reveal a wealth of hidden treasure. Maybe there is some truth in this because in 1985 the **Middleham Jewel** was discovered in a field close by. This 15th Century gold and sapphire pendant was sold for over £2.5 million in 1991 and is now housed in the Yorkshire Museum at York; there is a replica in the Castle Shop. The original castle was abandoned in 1180 when work began on a new stone **castle** with a massive Keep, one of the largest in England, which became known as the 'Windsor of the North'. Ownership passed to the powerful Neville family of Raby in 1270; this was their stronghold for over 200 years from where they ruled their vast Northern estates. Richard Neville, the Earl of Warwick (The Kingmaker), inherited the castle in 1461, which brought it firmly into the spotlight of National events, especially during the War of the Roses. Richard Plantaganet, later Richard III, grew up at the castle where he later met his wife Lady Anne Neville, the daughter of the Earl of Warwick. Their son Edward, Prince of Wales was born at the castle. Richard was granted Middleham after Warwick's death in 1471 and he became king in 1483 but was killed at the Battle of Bosworth in 1485. The castle remained Crown property until 1604 when it passed into private ownership and soon fell into disrepair and much of the stonework was plundered in the 17th Century to build local houses. I recommend a tour of the Castle to see the 12th Century Keep and Great Hall surrounded by high curtain walls - climb to the top of the Keep for wonderful views across lower Wensleydale. There are a number of old houses along the lane that runs parallel to the main road, including **Laundry House** with its large chimney. **Manor House,** which dates from the 17th Century although rebuilt in the Georgian period, has been the home of the Peacock family since 1884, one of Middleham's most famous racing families. They have trained scores of winners over the years including 'Dante' who won the Derby in 1945, the last horse trained in the North of England to do so; the Peacock family still own Manor House Stables to the rear of the house. Horse breeding and training can be traced back to the monks of Jervaulx Abbey, however it was during the 18th Century that racehorse training began to flourish as the wide open spaces of **Middleham High and Low Moors** provided the perfect gallops. This growth in racehorse training brought prosperity to the town and it was not long before a racecourse was laid out on High Moor, with races being held until 1873. Middleham remains a major centre for racehorse training and there are currently about 14 trainers and 300 horses in the town. Where the cobbled lane opens out into a small 'square' on the edge of the town, the ornate gates across to the right once led to **Middleham Hall,** a Jacobean house that was completely destroyed by fire in 1889. The present building was originally the servant's quarters and is now used as a farm and stud, owned by the Peacock family.

*3. Cross the road and turn back towards the town along the left-hand side of the road to reach the Swine Cross and Water Fountain in the small market place known as the Swine Market.*

The road quickly opens out into another small 'square' to your left overlooked by the old almshouses of the town. You then come to the **Swine Market,** once the town's livestock market, at the centre of which is the Swine Cross, also known as the Top Cross, a badly weathered carved stone 'animal' said to be a White Boar, the emblem of Richard III. This was erected to commemorate the grant of a twice-yearly market and fair by Richard III in 1479. Close by is a **Water Fountain** constructed to commemorate Queen Victoria's Golden Jubilee in 1887, with a bull ring set into the cobbles nearby. Overlooking this area is the **Old School** complete with bell tower, built in 1869 in memory of the Rev. James Birch, Rector of Middleham, by his parishoners and friends; it has housed the Old School Arts Workshop since 1981. Sundial House stands to the right of the Old School, once the town's Post Office, with an ornate sundial complete with Latin inscription dated '1778'.

4. *From the Swine Cross take the lane to the left of the Old School passing the Methodist Church on your left then as the lane bends round to the left take the path to the right through a stile and follow this down to reach the Church. Bear right through the churchyard then head through the lych gate and follow Church Street straight on to reach the main road (Kirkgate).*

**Middleham Church,** dedicated to St Mary and St Alkelda, dates back to the 13th Century, although the site has been used for worship since Saxon times. St Alkelda was a Saxon princess who was strangled by the Danes in the 9th Century because of her faith. The remains of a Saxon woman, thought to be St Alkelda, were found beneath the nave during restoration work in 1878 and a fragment of what is thought to be her tombstone has been set into the floor of the nave. The church is also noted for the elaborate tombstone of Robert Thornton, Abbot of Jervaulx, who died in 1533. The Church was made a collegiate foundation in 1478 by Richard III for a Dean and six secular priests, originally known as the King's College, Middleham. This College continued, although gradually diminishing in power, until 1845 when the status of Middleham as a 'Royal Peculiar' with ecclesiastical jurisdiction for the parish was abolished and then it became an ordinary Parish Church in 1856 when the last Dean died. As you walk along Church Street, note the house to your left (**Kingsley House**) which was once the Deanery and is now home to Mark Johnston racing stables, one of the country's top trainers. Where Church Street meets Kirkgate, the house opposite (**Warwick House**) was where Captain Neville Crump trained three Grand National winners.

**5.** *Walk down to the left along Kirkgate (which becomes Leyburn Road) to reach the brick-built Middleham Motors. Retrace your steps back up along Kirkgate into the Market Place.*

The building that now houses **Middleham Motors** was originally a cinema known as the 'Picture House Middleham', which opened in 1922 and finally closed in 1960; you can still see the old stage. The small area of land to the right immediately before Middleham Motors with trees and a small stream is known as the **Talking Well.** This was once the main source of water for the town and local women would come here to collect water and then stop for a chat! The stream rises above Middleham and flows through a culvert beneath the town As you head back up towards the Market Place you pass **Brief Cottage** on your right with a stone star shape above the door, ornate stonework and four unusual circular chimneys. Just before you reach the Market Place a cobbled lane leads up to the right to **Hepple House**, built in 1836 as a Methodist Chapel.

# Northallerton

| | |
|---|---|
| **TIME:** | Two hours |
| **START:** | Applegarth Car Park |
| **TOILETS:** | Applegarth Car Park |
| **CAFÉ:** | Several to choose from in the Town Centre; try Betty's - a Yorkshire institution! |
| **PUBS:** | Plenty of choice - try The Fleece Inn near the Town Hall. |
| **PARKING:** | Applegarth Car Park, just off the main High Street |
| **INFORMATION:** | Northallerton Tourist Information Centre: 01609 776864 |
| **MARKET DAYS:** | Wednesday and Saturday |

*"Northallerton was once renowned throughout England for its good, strong ale not to mention its extortionate prices – and that was back in the 18th Century! Indeed, in 1697 Giles Morrington wrote 'Northallerton, in Yorkshire, does excel All England, nay all Europe, for strong ale.'"*

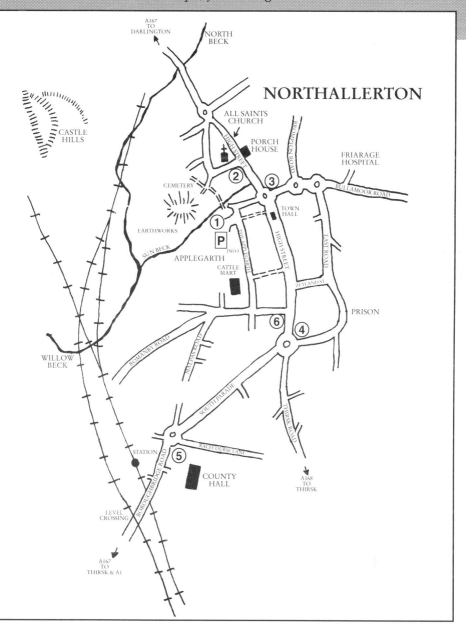

NORTHALLERTON

A167 TO DARLINGTON

NORTH BECK

CASTLE HILLS

ALL SAINTS CHURCH

PORCH HOUSE

HIGH STREET

BROMPTON ROAD

FRIARAGE HOSPITAL

BULLAMOOR ROAD

CEMETERY

EARTHWORKS

SUN BECK

TOWN HALL

EAST ROAD

APPLEGARTH

P INFO

THE APPLEGARTH

HIGH STREET

CATTLE MART

ZETLAND ST.

PRISON

WILLOW BECK

ROMANBY ROAD

MALPAS ROAD

SOUTH PARADE

THIRSK ROAD

A168 TO THIRSK

STATION

BOROUGHBRIDGE ROAD

RACECOURSE LANE

COUNTY HALL

LEVEL CROSSING

A167 TO THIRSK & A1

**1.** *From Applegarth Car Park head towards the church spire in the distance and cross the small footbridge to the left of the houses, then head along the path (enclosed by white railings) down to reach the gates to the cemetery and the Oddfellows Arms where you turn right to reach the Church and the High Street.*

Northallerton is a prosperous market town in the heart of the Vale of Mowbray, the County Town of the old North Riding of Yorkshire and now the administrative centre for North Yorkshire. This was also an important stop on the old coaching routes north, its long sweeping High Street is still lined with elegant Georgian buildings and ancient coaching inns. However, the history of Northallerton stretches back much further - it even had a Norman castle, Bishops' Palace and a 14th Century Carmelite Friary, as you will discover on this walk. Following the Norman Conquest, a wooden castle was built to the west of the town, probably on a site known as Howe Hill beside the River Wiske, although some authorities claim that it was situated at **Castle Hills.** There is evidence to suggest that Castle Hills was actually the site of a Roman camp or even a signal station as Roman remains were uncovered during construction of the railway line that cut through the site. This theory is supported by the fact that a Roman Road between York (Eboracum) and Hadrian's Wall ran just to the east of the town through Bullamoor. This early Norman castle was destroyed in the late 12th Century and a 'new' castle was built closer to the ancient Parish Church on a site now occupied by the large cemetery. This was the **Palace of the Bishops of Durham,** the famed 'Prince Bishops' that once ruled the North of England almost as a separate kingdom. The all powerful Bishops of Durham were granted the Manor of Allerton in the years following the Norman Conquest and it stayed with these Prince Bishops until 1836. In medieval times this palace entertained many important guests and Royalty including King John, Henry III and Edward I. During the 12th to 14th Centuries many Kings of England and their armies travelled through Northallerton on a number of occasions to fight the Scots; just to the north of the town is the site of the Battle of the Standard where the English forces inflicted heavy losses on the Scots in 1138. Following the political upheavals of the 16th and 17th Centuries, this fortified Palace fell into ruin, so that by the mid 18th Century no stonework remained. Extensive earthworks including a conical mound or 'motte' and overgrown moat can still be clearly seen amongst the gravestones and through trees beyond the cemetery. The **Parish Church of All Saints** looks out across an oasis of greenery with cottages and a pub overlooking a small green, giving it an almost rural appearance - this was where the markets were originally held. All Saints Church is of Norman origin, however this site was almost certainly used for worship in Pre-Conquest days as carved Saxon stones have been found. Indeed, it has been suggested that St Paulinus, Archbishop of York, built a simple church here in the 7th Century. The present Church retains some Norman work, but is predominantly Early English and Perpendicular, built under the guidance of the Bishops of Durham; the church was badly damaged by the Scots in the 14th Century. The building on the corner in front of the church gates was the site of **Northallerton Grammar School,** which can trace its foundation back to at least 1322 and retained close connections with Durham Cathedral for many Centuries. The present building dates from 1776 and was used as a school until 1906, when new premises were built in Grammar School Lane.

John A. Ives 101.

**2.** *At the junction with the main High Street, cross the road to reach Porch House and the Police Station then turn right down along the High Street to quickly reach a small roundabout.*

**Porch House,** to the left of the Police Station, is Northallerton's oldest house built in 1584 by the Metcalfe family, an influential and powerful Yorkshire family who owned the house for generations. Charles I stayed here in 1640 as a guest and again in 1647 as a prisoner whilst being brought down from Scotland by the Parliamentary Commissioners following the Civil War. The house on your left before the roundabout was known as **Vine House** and dates back to Tudor times, taking its name from a huge vine that once grew along the front of the houses - the circumference of its stem measured 3ft 11' and was said to be the largest vine in the country. The house became a cottage hospital in 1877 for eight patients and now houses the Rutson Rehabilitation Hospital, named after one of its benefactors. A short detour along the road to the left at the roundabout brings us to the **Friarage Hospital.** This hospital was established during the Second World War as a RAF Hospital, however it stands on the site of a 14th Century Carmelite Friary that was suppressed by Henry VIII; no trace of the monastic buildings remain. The white building on the right by the entrance is **Sunbeck House,** which was built in 1857 as the town's workhouse for 120 of the poorest people in the parish; the diminutive stream known as Sun Beck runs underneath the town and through Applegarth.

**3.** *Continue down the High Street passing the Town Hall down to reach the large roundabout at the bottom of the street.*

The brick-built **Town Hall** stands rather obtrusively in the middle of the High Street. Built in 1873 by the 'Market and Public Improvements Co Ltd' on the site of the old

Toll Booth and Shambles, or butchers' market, it now houses the offices of the Town Council as well as a number of shops. Adjacent to this is the old **Fleece Inn,** which stands on the site of an early 14th Century Austin Friary founded by William de Alverton in 1341, although no traces of this Friary remain. This fine stone and timber building still retains a great deal of the character that once charmed Charles Dickens. Further along the High Street is the 19th Century **Market Cross,** built to replace the ancient cross removed in the 1870's. Northallerton has been an important trading centre since Norman times as it lies at the junction of a number of busy routes in the fertile Vale of Mowbray. The town was granted the right to hold regular fairs by King John in 1200 and the weekly Wednesday street market has been a feature of the town since at least the 14th Century. The **Golden Lion Inn** is one of the town's finest buildings, its superb Georgian façade a distinctive feature of the High Street. The present inn dates from 1725, although an inn has stood on the site since Tudor times, and developed as a coaching inn and Posting House on the old Great North Road between London and Edinburgh. In the 17th Century the first Turnpike road (the Great North Road) was opened between London and York to improve the appalling condition of the roads and roughly followed the route of the old Roman Road north. In the mid 18th Century the route northwards to Edinburgh was improved and in 1745 the Boroughbridge to Durham Turnpike opened, which further increased the town's stature as an important coaching stop. At the height of the coaching era the Great North Road went from York through Boroughbridge, Northallerton, Durham, Newcastle to Edinburgh. A short detour to the left along **Zetland Street** brings us to the old **North Riding Registry of Deeds,** a fine Georgian building built in 1736 that was converted into the Registrar's house in 1782. In the early 18th Century there were only a couple of places in the country where deeds and other important documents could be registered and this was one of them - one of the main reasons why Northallerton developed into the County Town.

**4.** *At the roundabout take the road to the right (South Parade) and follow this down to reach County Hall and the Railway Station.*
The elegant tree-line street of **South Parade,** lined with Victorian villas and fine brick-built terraced houses, leads down to **County Hall.** This imposing building was built in 1906 to a design of the renowned local architect Walter Brierley as the administrative offices for the old North Riding of Yorkshire, which had been created in 1889. This Grade II* listed building has the appearance of a stately home with formal gardens, water features and an entrance hall with Belgian and Sicilian marble floors and a sweeping staircase. Over 1,000 people now work here looking after the county of North Yorkshire. County Hall actually stands on the site of Northallerton's **Racecourse,** laid out in 1765 and a popular amenity for visitors, however, when the railway was built through the town it cut through part of the Racecourse and this smaller course saw its last race in the 1880's. The **railway** arrived in Northallerton in 1841 heralding the end of the town's proud coaching tradition. Until the notorious

Beeching cuts of the 1960's you could catch a train from Northallerton to almost anywhere in the country including Ripon, Harrogate, Leyburn, Hawes, Middlesbrough, York and Darlington. It is still forms an important part of the rail network with the East Coast Mainline running through the town and there are efforts to reopen the Wensleydale Railway. The Station Hotel is a superb example of a late Victorian hotel dating from 1902 and retains many original features including ornate etched window glass and tiling and has kept its layout of several small rooms and corridors.

**5.** *Retrace your steps back along South Parade and left along the High Street then turn left along Romanby Road after the Durham Ox pub.*

The wide sweeping **High Street** is lined with elegant 18th and 19th Century buildings, although many frontages have been altered over the years - look above the shop fronts to see the original buildings. When the **Great North Road** passed through Northallerton in the 18th Century, the town prospered with numerous fine coaching inns opening to accommodate visitors and horses; many of these old inns retain their original façades. Northallerton was once renowned throughout England for its good, strong ale not to mention its extortionate prices - and that was back in the 18th Century! Indeed, in 1697 Giles Morrington wrote, "Northallerton, in Yorkshire, does excel All England, nay all Europe, for strong ale." Note the ancient oak crucks in the gable end of the Nags Head as you enter the High Street.

**6.** *Take the first turning on the right back towards the Applegarth, passing the livestock market on your left, then take the alleyway to the right immediately after the Zion United Reformed Church. Follow this up through Tickle Toby Yard to re-emerge on the High Street. Turn left heading back up the High Street then head to the left through one of the many arcades or alleyways back to the Car Park.*

**Applegarth** stands as one of the few open spaces in the town, through which flows the small stream that rises just to the east of the town. The trees that shade the footpath alongside the road were planted by members of the Town Council in 1937 to commemorate the Coronation of King George VI. The red-brick **Zion United Reformed Church** is housed in an old Sunday School that was built in 1858, next to which was Northallerton's **Georgian Theatre.** This building was used as a theatre from 1800 until 1832 and is where famous actors of their day such as Edmund Keen once performed, it was later used as a Methodist chapel up until 1889, how ironic that is now houses a pub! Northallerton boasts many high class and individual shops including **Betty's Tea Rooms** and **Barker's Store,** a renowned family-run department store that has served the needs of shoppers since 1875. Safeway's now occupies the **Old Golden Lion Inn,** a once famous 17th Century coaching inn, and Frank Clarkson's shop, a silversmith in the town who made the Mayor's Chain of Office.

# Pateley Bridge & Bewerley

## ⓘ ESSENTIAL WALK INFORMATION

| | |
|---|---|
| **TIME:** | Two & a half hours |
| **START:** | The bridge across the River Nidd at the bottom of the High Street. |
| **TOILETS:** | Car Park off the High Street also in the Recreation Ground across the River Nidd. |
| **CAFÉ:** | Wilding's Tea Rooms along Nidd Walk or Pateley Coffee House on the High Street. |
| **PUBS:** | The Crown, Talbot Hotel or the Royal Oak. |
| **PARKING:** | Pay & Display parking off the High Street and also Bewerley Park across the River Nidd. |
| **INFORMATION:** | Pateley Bridge Tourist Information Centre: 01423 711147 |

> *"At weekends the navvies who had worked all week on the dams came into town for a drink along with the local quarrymen, miners and mill-workers – by all accounts it was like the Wild West!"*

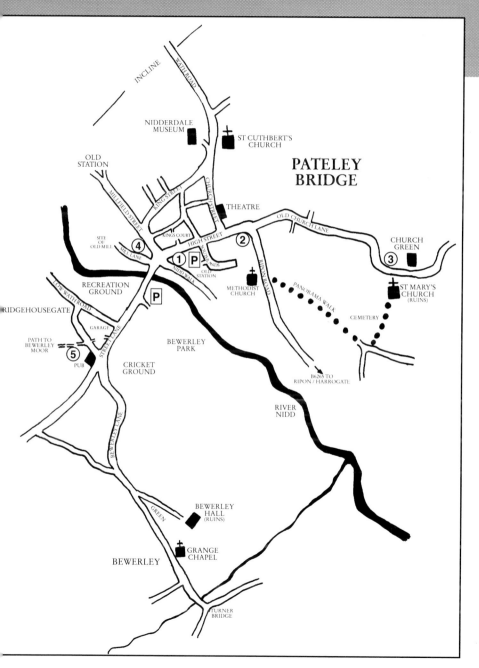

**PATELEY BRIDGE**

INCLINE

WATH ROAD

NIDDERDALE MUSEUM

ST CUTHBERT'S CHURCH

OLD STATION

MILLFIELD STREET

KING STREET

CHURCH STREET

THEATRE

OLD CHURCH LANE

CHURCH GREEN

SITE OF OLD MILL

MILL LANE

KINGS COURT

HIGH STREET

SOUTHWD

④

①

P

②

NIDD WALK

OLD STATION

③

ST MARY'S CHURCH (RUINS)

RECREATION GROUND

METHODIST CHURCH

NIDD ROAD

PANORAMA WALK

CEMETERY

LOW WATH ROAD

P

RIDGEHOUSEGATE

GARAGE

BEWERLEY PARK

⑤

PUB

PATH TO BEWERLEY MOOR

STREET LANE

CRICKET GROUND

B6265 TO RIPON / HARROGATE

RIVER NIDD

BEWERLEY LANE

GREEN

BEWERLEY HALL (RUINS)

GRANGE CHAPEL

BEWERLEY

TURNER BRIDGE

**1.** *From the bridge across the River Nidd in the centre of Pateley Bridge, walk up the High Street to reach the gardens at the top of the street where the road bends round to the right.*

There has been a river crossing at Pateley Bridge for possibly 2,000 years as it is thought that the Romans came this way to their lead mines on the moors around Greenhow. Initially there was a ford across the river, however a bridge was first recorded in 1320. Pateley Bridge grew in importance as it lay on the busy monastic road from Fountains Abbey over to Wharfedale as well as the old High Road to Craven. In the 18th and 19th Centuries a number of turnpike roads were established which, coupled with the local mines, quarries and mills, meant that the town soon became a bustling place. A short walk along **Nidd Walk** brings you to the old Station building that once formed the terminus of the **North Eastern Railway** branch line from the Harrogate to Ripon line, which opened in 1862, however passenger services were withdrawn in 1951 and it closed completely in 1964. This railway crossed the bottom of the High Street by way of a level crossing and met up with the **Nidd Valley Light Railway** beyond Millfield Street, which was operated by Bradford Corporation between 1907 and 1936 to service the construction of the two huge dams in upper Nidderdale. For a number of years this also provided a passenger service as far as Lofthouse, the only rail passenger service operated by a municipality in the country - remarkably, Pateley Bridge once had two stations. There are several buildings of note along the **High Street** including **David South Antiques**, which is housed in the old King's Arms pub, a fine Georgian coaching inn that called last orders in the 1960's. **King's Court** can be found through the coaching arch beside this old pub, a flagged courtyard with an array of small shops housed in the former stabling block. The **Crown Inn** has helped slake the thirst of locals since the 18th Century, however it was rebuilt in the late 19th Century following its acquisition by Metcalfe's Brewery. The elegant ivy-clad **Talbot Hotel** boasts an attractive frontage and dates from the 18th Century when it served as a coaching inn, then a pub and now a comfortable hotel. By the end of the 19th Century Pateley Bridge supported two breweries and several pubs, most of which have now closed. At weekends the navvies who had worked all week on the dams came into town for a drink along with the local quarrymen, miners and mill-workers - by all accounts it was like the Wild West! You soon come to a row of stone cottages on your left (the oldest houses in the town) that date back to the 17th Century on the corner of which is the **'Oldest Sweet Shop in England'**, established in 1827. On the right at the top of the High Street is **The Pateley Club** in a building that dates back to 1664 that was originally a pub known as the George Inn. In 1775 Elizabeth Metcalfe began brewing beer to supply this pub which she had inherited a few years earlier. Her brewery soon expanded to become a large commercial brewer known as **'The Nidderdale Brewery, J Metcalfe & Sons'** that produced a range of fine ales until it closed in 1912. The pub closed in the late 19th Century and became brewery offices then the Pateley Bridge Conservative Club, however most of the buildings have been demolished - the brewery stood at the top of the road on the right where the gardens are today.

**2.** *At the top of the High Street follow the main road (Ripon Road) round to the right passing the Methodist Church then take the path up to the left ('Panorama Walk') immediately after The Terrace on your left. Follow this enclosed path up to reach the gates of the cemetery, where you continue straight on up the lane for a short distance then turn to the left up some steps and follow the narrow walled path (with the cemetery on your left) to reach the ruins of St Mary's Church. Head straight on through the churchyard and onto the road.*

The distinctive tower of the **Methodist Church** rises up above the town, built in 1909 to replace an earlier chapel of 1777. John Wesley was a regular visitor to the town in the 18th Century and the original pulpit from where he preached still remains inside the church. Across the road is **The Terrace**, a Georgian house built by George and Elizabeth Metcalfe that hides behind a stone wall crowned by an ornate wrought iron lamp. The flagged path known as the **Panorama Walk** was the main road to Ripon and Fountains Abbey in medieval times. Note the old well by the side of the path with its large inscribed stone "I'll habits gather by unseen degrees, a brook run rivers and rivers run to seas. The way to the church." Just after the cemetery a walled path leads off this old highway towards **St Mary's Church** with views opening up across Nidderdale. As you enter the churchyard immediately to your right under an old yew tree is the grave of Mary Myers who lived to the ripe old age of 120 before she died in 1743. This lovely old church, now a roofless ruin, dates from the early 14th Century but was abandoned in the 19th Century as the town developed around the river crossing. This area is known as **Church Green** and was probably the site of the original settlement, indeed the name of the town is derived from the Anglo-Saxon word 'patleia' meaning a 'path through a clearing'.

**3.** *Turn left along the road and follow this steeply down to reach the junction at the top of the High Street. Continue straight on back into the town then take the turning to the right by the old Sweet Shop along Church Street to reach St Cuthbert's Church. Head straight on along Wath Road out of the town to reach the bridge above the old Incline, then retrace your steps back to the Church where you follow King Street down to the right and follow this all the way to reach the bridge across the River Nidd at the bottom of the High Street.*

The old three-storey buildings on the right just before the junction at the top of the High Street were once used by Metcalfe's Brewery as a store and stabling. Note the old water trough on the right, known as the **Souter Well**, dated 1852 with a fox's head for a water spout; this well originally stood at the foot of the Panorama Walk. Just along **Church Street** is **The Playhouse** with its elegant Doric columns and portico, built in 1859 as a Primitive Methodist Chapel before being used by the Salvation Army and finally the Pateley Bridge Dramatic Society as a small theatre. Next door is the **Oddfellows Hall,** another fine mid 19th Century building where the Order of Oddfellows would meet, a Friendly Society that offered its members (mainly local miners and quarrymen) insurance against ill health or injury before the days of National Insurance. **St Cuthbert's Parish Church** was built in 1828 to replace St Mary's Church and has a spacious but simple interior. Inside the entrance area is a 15th Century bell that originally came from Fountains Abbey. Further along Wath Road on the outskirts of the town is a bridge above the old **Incline,** a steep railway built in 1876 to transport stone from the Scotgate Ash Quarries further up the hillside to the railway along the valley floor. This quarry was noted for the quality of its flagstones, which were used throughout the country during the 19th Century for the steps of many grand buildings as well as piers and railway platforms; the quarries closed in the 1920's. Situated at the top of **King Street** is the award-winning **Nidderdale Museum,** housed in the former Victorian workhouse. This imposing building with its two protruding gable ends was built in 1863 to provide shelter for the needy of the area, however it closed in 1914 although the Vagrant Ward continued to be used until the Second World War. **Millfield Street,** with its rows of Victorian terraced houses built for the quarrymen and millworkers, leads down to the old **Nidd Valley Light Railway Station** (private). The stone bridge across the **River Nidd** dates from the 18th Century, and was enlarged in the 19th Century. Immediately before the bridge on the right is **Mill Lane** that leads down to the site of an old corn mill, of which only some millworkers' cottages remain. In the 18th and 19th Centuries there were at least forty mills along the banks of the Nidd between upper Nidderdale and Knaresborough processing flax, corn, rope, and cotton - Nidderdale was once famous for its linen weaving. By the 1960's most of these mills had closed.

**4.** *Cross over the bridge and head straight on along Street Lane passing the Recreation Ground on your right then turn right along Low Wath Road. Follow this road down for a short distance then take the first turning to the left almost back on yourself ('Dead End / No Entry' road signs) and follow this back to reach Street Lane by the Royal Oak pub.*

The area across the bridge is known as **Bridgehousegate.** Across to the right is the large **Recreation Ground** with its attractive gardens, bowling green and bandstand. To the left is **Bewerley Park,** the home of the Nidderdale Show every September organised by the Nidderdale Agricultural Society, founded in 1895. This annual show can be traced back to the early 1300's when Pateley Bridge was given the right to hold a weekly market and an annual fair - the market died out about 100 years ago but the fair survives as the Nidderdale Show. Situated along the back lane through Bridgehousegate is a wonderful stone-built Victorian 'tower brewery' - ingredients go in at the top (water, malt, hops, yeast) and beer comes out at the bottom. A member of the Metcalfe family set this brewery up after a family row. Further on are some new houses called Chapel Mews Cottages where an **Independents Chapel** (later the United Reformed Church) once stood; the gravestone of Nathan Newbould can still be found set into the wall of the alleyway to the left.

**5.** *At the road take the lane diagonally opposite to the right and follow this up into Bewerley. Walk through the village passing the 'green' on your left to reach Bewerley Grange Chapel. Retrace your steps back to the main road by the Royal Oak pub where you turn right back into Pateley Bridge.*

**Bewerley** is a lovely village with attractive 18th Century cottages facing onto a small green complete with a red 'phone box, mature trees and an old water trough still with a working tap. The monks of Fountains Abbey held extensive lands in Nidderdale in medieval times and had a farm, or grange, here. Hidden away along the road through the village is **Bewerley Grange Chapel,** built between 1494 and 1526 by Marmaduke Huby, one of the last Abbots of Fountains Abbey before the Dissolution of the Monasteries by Henry VIII. On the far gable end of this simple chapel is a carved Latin inscription that translates as "To the only God be honour and glory for ever" with the initials M.H. - this was the motto of Abbot Huby, which can also be found inscribed on the side of the Tower at Fountains Abbey.

# Pickering

**TIME:** Two hours

**START:** At the top of the Market Place.

**TOILETS:** Eastgate Car Park or along The Ropery

**CAFÉ:** Several to choose from; try Mulberries Coffee Shop along Bridge Street, Russell's Café in the Market Place or the Tea Rooms along Burgate.

**PUBS:** Plenty of choice; try the White Swan Hotel or the Bay Horse in the Market Place.

**PARKING:** Large car parks off Eastgate and The Ropery.

**INFORMATION:** Pickering Tourist Information Centre: 01751 47379

**MARKET DAY:** Monday

> *"It is true to say that people have been living in this area for many thousands of years, indeed according to legend Pickering was founded over 2,000 years ago by Pereduras, King of the native British tribe in this area. Apparently he lost his favourite ring whilst swimming in a nearby river and later found it inside a pike which had been cooked for his dinner!"*

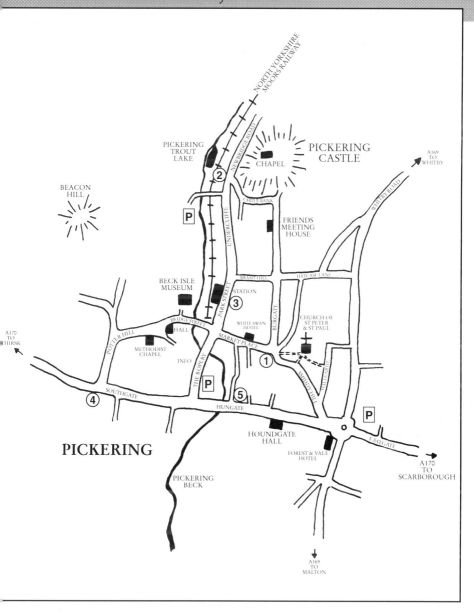

97

1. *From the top of the Market Place walk up Burgate to reach Pickering Castle. Follow the road (Castle Bank) down to the left then round to the right and head down the steps to the left after the last houses to reach Park Street / Undercliffe.*

**Burgate,** originally Boroughgate, was once the main route up to the castle from the town and is lined with a variety of buildings ranging from rather grand Victorian houses to older cottages. It was along this street that Marfitt's tallow candle-making workshop was located, a wonderful relic of a Victorian workshop that has since been moved to the Castle Museum at York. **Castle Cinema** is a reminder of days gone by - originally opened in 1937 it appears to have changed little over the years although I hope the films have! Whilst walking up this street, look out for the old 'Preaching Stone' outside **Melbury House** (No. 30), on which Primitive Methodist preachers once stood to address the townsfolk; John Wesley visited the town on a number of occasions and may have used this stone. **Brant Hill,** local dialect for a steep hill, leads down to the Station and Pickering Beck from where water was brought up to the town in the days before running tap water. Further up this street is the **Friends' Meeting House,** which lies hidden away amongst peaceful gardens that are also a Quaker burial ground; in the Quaker tradition the gravestones just recall the person's name and the year they were born and died. This rather grand building was built in 1793 - many Meeting Houses are much smaller and simpler. A sign outside the Meeting House talks of Quakers and Peace: *"We actively oppose all that leads to violence among people and nations, and violence to other species and to our planet. Refusal to fight with weapons is not surrender."* Note the large stone mounting blocks situated at the end of the long row of old cottages. **Pickering Castle** is a superb example of a 'motte and bailey' castle and dates back to 1069 when William the Conqueror ordered a wooden castle to be built to subdue the unruly North and also act as a centre from where the vast Honour of Pickering could be administered. This Honour was a huge tract of land stretching as far as Goathland in the north and across to the coast that provided food, provisions and resources for the Castle as well as the Crown - this was all owned by William the Conqueror, much of which remain with the Crown to this day. Although its walls were rebuilt in stone during the 13th and 14th Centuries, the Castle saw little military action and developed primarily as a hunting lodge for medieval Kings to hunt deer and wild boar in the surrounding Royal Forest of Pickering; between 1100 and 1400 every King of England visited this castle. This Forest was a hunting preserve within the Honour of Pickering and was governed by strict Forest Laws and courts were held at the Castle for anyone found in breach of them. In 1361 the Castle passed into the ownership of **John of Gaunt** who was made the Duke of Lancaster in the following year, a title that brought with it vast estates and castles including Pickering. His grandson became King Henry V in 1413 and the Duchy of Lancaster reverted to the Crown where it remains to this day.

From the 15th Century onwards the Castle began to fall into disrepair, as its main function was the management of the Forest and estates rather than military use. Unlike many northern castles, Pickering suffered not at the hands of Parliamentarians during the Civil War, but from stonemasons who plundered the ruins to build houses for the local gentry. The ruins of Pickering Castle are impressive with the incredible conical motte in the heart of the ruins, from where there are wonderful views across the red roofs of the town towards the North York Moors. Of particular note is **Beacon Hill**, which lies across the railway lines above the playing fields. As the name suggests, this has been used as a signal station for centuries to warn of invasions such as the Spanish Armada or to celebrate events such as Victory at Waterloo and Queen Elizabeth II's Silver Jubilee. It is thought that it may have also been the site of a prehistoric fortification. It is true to say that people have been living in this area for many thousands of years, indeed according to legend Pickering was founded over 2,000 years ago by Pereduras, King of the native British tribe in this area. Apparently he lost his favourite ring whilst swimming in a nearby river and later found it inside a pike which had been cooked for his dinner!

**2.** *Turn left along Park Street and follow this down to reach Pickering Station on your right.*

A lane leads off Park Street across a stone bridge and level crossing into the parking area for the railway and the Pickering Trout Lake. This small stone bridge actually spans a mill race that once provided the power for the undershot waterwheel of **High Mill,** the large three-storey mill that fronts Park Street. **Pickering Station** is home to the North Yorkshire Moors Railway, which offers a glimpse of the 'golden age of steam' with beautifully preserved stations, carriages, locomotives and 18 miles of track through the heart of the North York Moors. The railway was completed in 1836 and connected Pickering with Whitby to provide a stimulus for its flagging whaling and shipbuilding industries. Designed by George Stephenson, this was one of the first passenger railways in the world, although the carriages were initially horse-drawn. George Hudson, the 'Railway King' bought the line in 1845 and set about upgrading it for locomotive use and extended it to join up with the York to Scarborough line at Rillington. Following the Beeching Report, this railway was controversially closed in 1965, however the **North Yorkshire Moors Railway Preservation Society** was formed in 1967 and subsequently reopened the line between Grosmont and Pickering to the public in 1973 as a preserved steam railway. The Station is a wonderful example of an early Victorian station, built in 1845 following the acquisition of the line by George Hudson. The fine stone walls once supported a roof, however this was dismantled in the 1950's. In the days when the railway went all the way to Rillington, it crossed The Ropery and Hungate by way of level crossings - there are plans to reinstate this section of track to link the historic North Yorkshire Moors Railway once again to the York to Scarborough line.

**3.** *Continue along Park Street then turn right after the Station into Bridge Street. Follow this road across the bridge over Pickering Beck then head straight on up Potter Hill following the road round to the left down to reach Southgate.*

The large building on the left as you turn along Bridge Street was once a **Primitive Methodist Chapel** that was built in 1851 but replaced over thirty years later by a larger chapel on Potter Hill. It was later used as a theatre, Salvation Army citadel and a cinema before becoming a large gift and craft shop. Doctrinal disputes between different sections of the Methodist movement caused many rifts in the early 19th Century, indeed the Primitive Methodists and the Wesleyan Methodists were separate denominations until they united in 1932, along with the United Methodist Church, to form the Methodist Church of today. After the bridge on the right is the famous **Beck Isle Museum of Rural Life,** housed in a fine Georgian building that was owned by William Marshall during the late 18th and early 19th Centuries. Marshall was a pioneer of modern farming and introduced the idea of a Ministry of

Agriculture. He modified this building during the early 19th Century with the intention of establishing a College of Agriculture, but sadly died in 1818 before the project came to fruition; the two large arched windows were designed to allow plenty of light into his lecture room. The building now houses a fascinating Museum of Rural Life with thirty-one differently themed rooms from the Victorian era. The grassy area between the museum and the bridge is an oasis of tranquillity right in the heart of the town, although it is prone to flooding after heavy rain; the lower part of the bridge is medieval. Across the road from here is the **Memorial Hall** that was converted from an old mill into a large hall during the 1920's in memory of the local men who lost their lives during the Great War. The **Primitive Methodist Chapel** of 1885 dominates Potter Hill, built to replace the old chapel at the foot of Bridge Street - this was the third Primitive Methodist Chapel in the town. **Potter Hill** has a good mixture of house styles with Georgian, Victorian, Edwardian and post war. Around the corner from here is an old-fashioned fish and chip shop or, as they say in Yorkshire, a chip 'ole!

4. *Turn left along Southgate to reach the traffic lights at the road junction. Turn left here along The Ropery then head right at the crossroads up into the Market Place. Walk up through the Market Place and head right (almost opposite the Bay Horse) down Champley's Yard to reach Hungate.*

Pickering **Working Mens' Club** was once the Methodist Day School, how ironic that it is now a social club serving beer! Across to your right is **Coopers Store,** a family-run business that dates back to 1895. This store, formerly the Drill Hall, sells just about everything and is deceptively large, stretching back a very long way from its relatively narrow front. Further down the street is a lovely terrace of Victorian houses, many retaining their original features; typical is 'Southfield View'. Across to your right from the traffic lights is the old brick-built Engine Shed whilst The Ropery Car Park was once the Goods Yard and railway sidings. The lovely stone building on your left along **The Ropery** with its fine arched windows and small window panes was built as part of George Hudson's improvements to the line in the 1840's and was originally a warehouse and goods shed; it is now a hair stylists! The gently rising **Market Place** is home to many old fashioned shops and inns in particular the **Bay Horse,** where Parliamentary soldiers were billeted during the Civil War. The award-winning **White Swan Hotel** dates back to the 16th Century and later served as a coaching inn on the busy routes from York to Whitby and Scarborough; this was where smuggled salt was hidden, once a valuable commodity. Dominating the upper part of the Market Place is the **Conservative Club,** an imposing brick-built house that was built originally for Nicholas Piper, who made his fortune through whaling ships that sailed out of Whitby in the 18th Century.

*5. Turn left along Hungate then just before the roundabout at the main road junction, turn left up Smiddy Hill. Where the road bends round to the left along Birdgate at the top of this hill, head up the steps to the right to reach the Parish Church. Walk to the left through the churchyard back into the Market Place.*

In the days when the streets were open sewers, **Hungate** was where the leftover offal from the butchers' shops in the Market Place was dumped - the resulting mêlée of scavenging hounds gave this street its name. The **Kirk Theatre**, set back slightly from Hungate, is housed in a former Wesleyan Chapel that is now home to the Pickering Musical Society. There are numerous alleys and stables up to the left, a reminder of the days when Pickering was a halting point for stagecoaches between Leeds, York and the East Coast. The large whitewashed building across to the right is **Houndgate Hall,** which was once the home of Dr Kirk who collected many everyday items of 19th Century life whilst on his doctor's rounds throughout the southern North York Moors. The artefacts went on to form the famous Kirk Collection and are now on show at the Castle Museum at York. This Hall was also used as 'Skeldale House' in the film version of James Herriot's 'All Creatures Great and Small'. The **Forest and Vale Hotel** was built in 1787 as a mansion house known as Low Hall. There has been a hall on this site since medieval times when it was owned by the influential Hastings family, who at one time held the position of Constable of the Castle and Foresters of the Royal Forest; the house became a hotel in the early 1900's. **Smiddy Hill,** named after a blacksmiths' shop that once stood at the foot of the hill, was where the cattle market used to be held. Up to your right is the fine red brick **Liberal Club** of 1909. The development of Non-Conformist religions such as Methodism went hand in hand with the growth of Liberalism in the area, indeed in 1931 David Lloyd-George visited the town to support a local candidate. The **Black Swan** is an ancient coaching inn that has witnessed two major celebrations in connection with the North Yorkshire Moors Railway and also hosted Charles Dickens who stayed here in 1844. At the bottom of the steps leading into the churchyard is **Birdgate House,** an elegant bow-fronted Georgian building. The **Church of St Peter and St Paul** has its origins in Saxon times although it was replaced in about 1140 by a Norman church, with alterations and rebuilding works in the 13th and 14th Centuries. The Church is famous for its **medieval frescoes,** which are the finest and most complete wall paintings in England. These were painted in about 1460 to allow the illiterate congregation understand stories from the Bible. They were covered over during the Reformation and lay hidden beneath layers of plaster until they were rediscovered in 1852, only to be covered over again until 1876 by the vicar who feared idolatrous parishioners. The most striking images are of St George slaying the Dragon, the beheading of John the Baptist and the Descent into Hell.

# Richmond

**TIME:** Two hours

**START:** Town Hall, Richmond Market Place.

**TOILETS:** Market Place, Friary Gardens, The Green and The Fosse Car Park (Millgate).

**CAFÉ:** Several to choose from in and around the Market Place.

**PUBS:** Numerous pubs throughout the town - try the King's Head Hotel.

**PARKING:** The Market Place offers limited parking; there is also a large car park off Victoria Road.

**INFORMATION:** Richmond Tourist Information Centre: 01748 850252

**MARKET DAY:** Saturday

*"The town is set high above the River Swale, the fastest flowing river in England, which at this point flows through a dramatic ravine with sheer cliffs; indeed the name of the town comes from the Norman French 'riche' and 'mont' meaning 'strong hill' - of the many Richmonds throughout the world, North Yorkshire's was the first."*

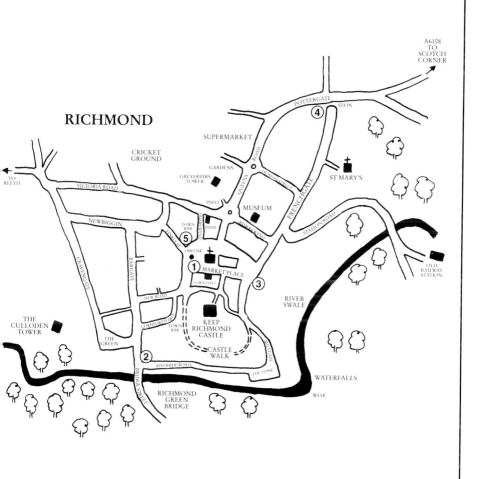

RICHMOND

**1.** *From the Town Hall and entrance to Richmond Castle (with Holy Trinity Church facing you) head left out of the corner of the Market Place onto Castle Hill. Follow New Road as it bends steeply down to the right then almost immediately take the cobbled lane to the left (The Bar) and follow this down through the Postern Gate then down Cornforth Hill to reach Bridge Street. Turn left along this road passing The Green to your right down to reach Richmond Green Bridge.*

Richmond is undoubtedly one of the finest towns in England, dominated by the incredible ruins of its castle built following the Norman Conquest with its massive stone Keep rising 100-feet above the Market Place. The town is set high above the River Swale, the fastest flowing river in England, which at this point flows through a dramatic ravine with sheer cliffs; indeed the name of the town comes from the Norman French 'riche' and 'mont' meaning 'strong hill' - of the many Richmonds throughout the world, North Yorkshire's was the first. During the 18th Century Richmond became somewhat of a fashionable resort for wealthy visitors and is famous for its many elegant Georgian houses. Following the Norman Conquest, William the Conqueror gave Alan Rufus, one of his loyal supporters, vast tracts of land centred on the northern Yorkshire Dales, which collectively became known as the Honour of Richmond; he was also made the Earl of Richmond. In 1070 he ordered a castle to be built on cliffs above the River Swale from where he could administer his lands and subdue the unruly tribes of Northern Britain. This was the first **Norman castle** to be built of stone in this country, although the massive Keep was added 100 years later by his great nephew. The Castle never saw any military action and fell into disrepair during the 16th Century, however it returned to military use during the 19th Century when soldiers were stationed here. Large barracks were built within the grounds in 1855 and between 1908 and 1910 **General Robert Baden-Powell,** the founder of the Scout movement, was the commanding officer of the Territorial Army based here; the barracks were demolished in 1935. The Castle was also used as a prison for POW's as well as conscientious objectors during the Great War - this was where the famous **'Richmond 16'** were held, some of the first people to defy conscription on moral grounds. The Castle is noted for Scolland's Hall, one of the earliest domestic Norman buildings in the country, the sheer cliffs above the Swale and the imposing Keep. The climb to the top of the Keep is more than compensated by the views across the rooftops towards the Pennines. According to legend **King Arthur** and his Knights lie asleep in a cave beneath the Keep waiting for when their country needs them once more. The civilian town of Richmond developed alongside the Norman castle, with the earliest settlements in Newbiggin and Frenchgate, however houses soon began to be built within the castle's outer bailey (the present day Market Place) and Richmond quickly established itself as a trading centre gaining a Market Charter in 1093. The large **Obelisk** was constructed in 177? and replaced the town's ancient Market Cross. Despite the decline in the importance of the castle from the 16th Century onwards, Richmond prospered during the 18th and 19th Centuries as a commercial centre for the booming lead mining and woollen hand-knitting industries of the Dales as well as the fledgling tourist industry

Richmond's attractive cobbled **Market Place** is one of the largest and finest in England, lined with three-storey Georgian buildings. The 12th Century **Holy Trinity Church** stands proudly in the centre of the Market Place, originally built as a Chapel of Ease within the castle grounds and now the Regimental Headquarters and home of the Green Howards Regimental Museum, one of the country's oldest regiments founded in 1688. One of the town's most famous legends is that of the **Drummer Boy.** Many years ago a passage was found beneath the Market Place and a little drummer boy was lowered down into it. He then marched through the passage whilst soldiers and townsfolk followed the sound of the drum above ground for a considerable distance towards Easby Abbey until it suddenly stopped. Sadly, the boy was never seen again although the soft sound of his drum can sometimes be heard in the town. As you leave the Market Place along Castle Hill a lane leads off to the left just before New Road turns down to the right. This is the **Castle Walk** that was laid out in 1782 as a fashionable Georgian promenade beneath the Castle ramparts. Our route along **The Bar** takes us to one of two Postern Gates still to be found. The civilian town of Richmond was undefended until the Town Walls were built in 1312 due to the threat of Scottish raids. This stoutly built gate allowed pedestrian access into the town from the bridge across the Swale and was once a busy route into Richmond via **Cornforth Hill.** The house on the corner of Bridge Street and **The Green** has two rare Georgian sundials dating from 1720 and a '1689' date-stone above the door; the only surviving dated doorway in Richmond of the type found in Swaledale. The area known as The Green was the industrial district of Richmond in medieval times due to its proximity to the river with mills, a dyeworks and a brewery.

**2.** *Take the road to the left immediately before the bridge and follow this down with the river on your right to reach the weir and waterfalls at an area known as The Fosse. Continue along the road climbing steeply back up into the Market Place along Millgate.*

**Richmond Green Bridge** was built in the 1780's to a design of the famous architect John Carr and replaced a much older bridge. This was for many Centuries the only crossing of the river and was the start of the Richmond to Lancaster Turnpike. From the centre of the bridge there is perhaps the finest view of the Castle set majestically above the river, a scene that inspired Turner to capture it on canvas. The walk alongside the river is a delight with a dramatic series of waterfalls at **The Fosse.** There were several flour and corn mills in this area in medieval times including the Castle Mill and was later the site of Richmond Gas Works, which opened in 1820 as one of first public gas suppliers in Europe. The steep climb back up into the town affords wonderful views of the Keep rising above the jumble of cottages and alleyways, or wynds.

**3.** *Head straight on across the bottom end of the Market Place and out along Frenchgate, which you follow down to reach the road junction with Station Road. Continue straight on along the road then as the main road swings up to the left head on along the cobbled road ahead (still Frenchgate).*

This first section of **Frenchgate** was known as The Channel as many years ago water and sewage flowed down from the sloping Market Place along an open sewer in the street. This was also one of the main roads into the town in medieval times protected by the Frenchgate Bar, a large gate in the Town Walls which was sadly pulled down in the 1770's. A short detour to the left along Ryders Wynd takes you to the **Richmondshire Museum,** a fascinating museum dedicated to the history of the Richmondshire District and its people with displays such as the vet's surgery from BBC TV's 'All Creatures Great & Small and a wonderful model of Richmond Station. Frenchgate boasts many fine houses including **Grove House,** a superb brick-built Georgian house built in 1750 for Caleb Readshaw, a wealthy Richmond merchant who made his fortune selling hand-knitted woollen products from the Dales. The upper part of Frenchgate is perhaps the finest street in Richmond with elegant Georgian buildings overlooking a gently sloping cobbled street. No.24 was the home of **Robert Willance** who famously escaped death when his horse galloped over the edge of Whitcliffe Scar to the west of the town in 1606 at a spot still known as Willance's Leap. No. 83 was the birthplace of **John Fenwick** (1846 - 1905) who was also educated in the town. John Fenwick later worked as a draper at Stockton and Newcastle and founded the famous Fenwick's stores in Newcastle and London in 1882. **Church Wynd** leads down to the **Parish Church of St Mary.** Dating back to the 12th Century, the church was extensively restored in the 19th Century and is famous for its carved woodwork brought here from nearby Easby Abbey following the Dissolution of the Monasteries.

4. *Climb the steps at the top of Frenchgate up onto Pottergate, where you turn left heading back into town (Pottergate soon becomes Queen's Road) until you come to the second roundabout at the junction with Victoria Road and King Street (Friary Gardens on your right). At the roundabout turn right along Victoria Road then head left after the Georgian Theatre Royal along Friars Wynd that takes you back into the Market Place.*

**Queen's Road** was renamed after it had been widened in 1887, the year of Queen Victoria's Golden Jubilee, to create easier access into the Market Place. The formal lawns and flowerbeds of **Friary Gardens** are dominated by **Greyfriars Tower.** This gaunt tower dates from around 1500 and is all that remains of the Church of the Grey Friars, a small Franciscan friary that was founded in 1258 just outside the castle limits. Richmond's unique **Georgian Theatre Royal** is the oldest working theatre in its original form in the country, built in 1788 by Samuel Butler. There are daily tours where you can see the tiny boxes and benches as well as the stage, which appears to be bigger than the seating area - the theatre only holds 186 people! There is also a museum with the largest collection of Georgian theatre scenery in the country. A passage known as **Friars Wynd** leads from the side of the Theatre back into the Market Place, an ancient thoroughfare that gave access from the Market Place to the Friary where the townsfolk also collected their water from springs. Remnants of the 14th Century Town Walls can be seen here in the form of another Postern Gate. The tram-lines date from the late 19th Century and were laid by Robert Spence to transport goods from his ironmonger's shop in the Market Place to warehouses off Friars Wynd.

John A. Ives '01

**5.** *Turn right through the Market Place then turn right along Finkle Street and follow this down until it joins Newbiggin. Turn left into Newbiggin then take the first road down to the left along Bargate. Where the cobbled road meets the main road (tarmac) turn left and follow New Road steeply back up into the Market Place.*

**Finkle Street** was once one of the main routes into the town guarded by the medieval Finkle Bar that allowed access through the 14th Century Town Walls; the Bar was pulled down in 1773. **Newbiggin** means 'new settlement', as this was the site of one of the original civilian settlements in the 11th Century outside the castle's outer bailey. Today, it is a delightful area with a cobbled square and a wealth of elegant Georgian buildings. Of particular note is **The Unicorn,** an 18th Century coaching inn that boasts a rare letterbox inside that was used to collect mail before the red pillar-boxes were introduced. John Wesley, the founder of Methodism, is said to have preached from the steps of **Christmas House** with its ornate blue and white Georgian doorway. I recommend a detour along Newbiggin to admire the variety of buildings that line this tree-shaded cobbled street, at the end of which is the old **Police Station** that stands on the site of the old Richmond Gaol. It was here in 1558 that 'Protestant Martyrs' Richard and John Snell were imprisoned with Richard subsequently being burnt at the stake because he would not renounce his religious beliefs. **Bargate,** as the name suggests, provided access up to the Finkle Bar from the south; note the Board Inn, which has a very plain exterior with few windows as it was originally used as a food store and warehouse. **New Road** was built in the late 18th Century to provide better access into the Market Place replacing the ancient route up Cornforth Hill.

# Ripon

**TIME:** Two hours

**START:** Ripon Market Place.

**TOILETS:** Adjacent to the Tourist Information Centre

**CAFÉ:** Several to choose from in the City Centre.

**PUBS:** Plenty of choice - try the One Eyed Rat along Allhallowgate or The Unicorn Hotel in the Market Place.

**PARKING:** Large car parks off the main Market Place.

**INFORMATION:** Tourist Information Centre: Ripon 01765 604625; Harrogate 01423 537300.

**MARKET DAY:** Thursday

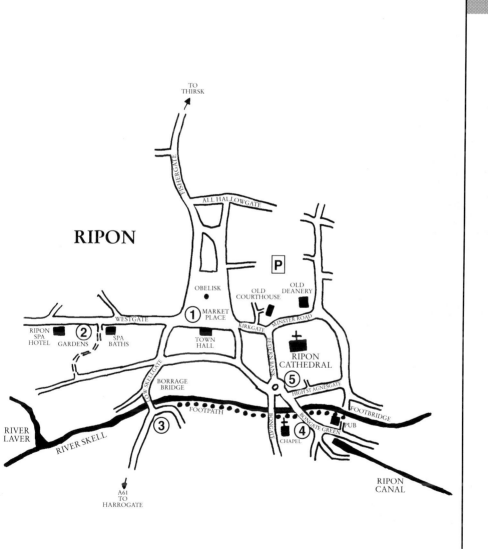

**1.** *From the Market Place head out of the corner of the square passing the Wakeman's House and follow Westgate all the way to reach Ripon Spa Baths.*

Ripon is more than a Market Town, as its incredible Cathedral merits city status, although it is still one of the smallest cities in England. Monks first settled here in the 7th Century and chose a site near to the confluence of the Rivers Skell, Laver and Ure. From this small monastic community a larger settlement soon grew as Ripon's importance as a trading centre developed due to its location on the edge of the Yorkshire Dales and the fertile Vale of York. The years following the Norman Conquest saw the city cement its status as an important centre for commerce with the construction of a wonderful new Cathedral under the direction of the Archbishop of York. Ripon's large **Market Place** retains its medieval layout with many 'gates' or streets leading from its four corners and narrow alleys threading their way between the buildings. There has been a weekly market held in this square since the city was granted a Market Charter in 1108, about the same time as the present Market Place was laid out to the west of the Cathedral by the Archbishop of York, who was also the Lord of the Manor. The most striking feature is the 90-ft slender stone **Obelisk,** erected in the 18th Century to replace the old market cross and is claimed to be the tallest and oldest free standing obelisk in the country. At 9pm every night the **Hornblower** sets the watch by sounding his horn at each corner of the obelisk, a tradition that can trace its origins to 886AD. Originally the Hornblower was known as the **Wakeman** who was charged, along with his constables, with keeping watch over the citizens of Ripon during the night - the Wakeman used to charge a fee to householders as a kind of insurance against burglary. The tradition of blowing the horn to set the watch has continued through the Centuries, although the title of Wakeman was changed to Mayor by Royal Charter in 1604. There are several interesting old buildings around the Market Place including the **Unicorn Hotel,** an old coaching inn frequented by King Edward VII and also where Tom Crudd, known as Old Boots, worked as a servant. His claim to fame was the ability to hold a coin between his nose and chin! The imposing **Town Hall** with its columns and clock has an eye-catching inscription: 'Except ye Lord keep ye Cittie ye Wakeman waketh in vain'. This building was designed by James Wyatt and built between 1799 and 1801, originally to house the Public Assembly and Reading Rooms. In 1897 the Marquess of Ripon gave the building to the city when it became the Town Hall; it still houses the offices of Ripon City Council and Harrogate Borough Council. One of the city's most famous buildings is the half-timbered **Wakeman's House,** which dates back to the 16th Century. For many years it was thought that this was the home of Sir Hugh Ripley, the last Wakeman although there has been much doubt thrown on this claim and it is now thought that the house was originally built as part of a larger medieval building. **Westgate** is home to many small and interesting shops as well as some rather fine Georgian and Victorian buildings.

**2.** *After the Spa Baths head left through the Spa Gardens towards the far left-hand corner of the gardens to join a path / steps that lead down to the road (Skellbank). Turn left along the road then at the crossroads turn right along Low Skellgate down to reach Borrage Bridge across the River Skell.*

**Ripon Spa Baths** were built in 1904 as a Pump Room when the popularity of 'spa treatment' was at its height - mineral water was piped from Grantley several miles away. The **Spa Gardens** were laid out around the same time as an area where wealthy Edwardians could stroll after 'taking the waters' and boast attractive gardens, bandstand and bowling green. Ripon tried, but sadly failed, to emulate the success of the neighbouring town of Harrogate, whose spa became world famous. The Spa Baths were converted into a swimming pool in the 1930's. The **Ripon Spa Hotel** opened in 1906 when Christopher Furness MP developed his grand house into a comfortable hotel to provide visitors to the Spa Baths with high-class accommodation. The hotel has been in the same family since 1929 and still boasts wonderful gardens and a genteel atmosphere of days gone by. **Borrage Bridge** carries the busy A61 into the city, although the new Ripon by-pass has reduced the queues of traffic somewhat. The striking riverside mill was home to **T & R Williamson** "Varnish and Enamel Works 1775", one of the most important employers in the city at one time. This now redundant building is currently being renovated into apartments.

**3.** *Cross Borrage Bridge then turn left along the road immediately after the bridge and follow the path alongside the River Skell that leads down to reach Bondgate Bridge. Cross the road and continue straight on along the riverside path down to reach the next stone bridge (Bondgate Green Bridge) and head up onto the road.*

A delightful path along the banks of the **River Skell** quickly takes you to **Bondgate Bridge**. Just to the right of this bridge is the **Hospital and Chapel of St John the Baptist**, a humble stone chapel founded in 1109. Ripon had three medieval ecclesiastical hospitals, which provided shelter for the poor of the city as well as impoverished travellers - the road that passes this chapel and crosses the River Skell is an ancient route between Ripon and Knaresborough. The chapel was restored in Victorian times when a row of almshouses was also built. This whole area just to the south of the river is known as **Bondgate** and was a separate settlement from Ripon years ago, but has now been swallowed up into the city. When you reach **Bondgate Green Bridge,** a short detour to the right will take you to the **Ripon Canal** - turn right along the road then take the first turning on the right then immediately left at the Navigation pub along Canal Road to reach the canal basin. Note the lovely row of Georgian brick-built terraced houses to the right near the bridge. This famous canal opened in 1773 and provided a pulse of life for Ripon until the arrival of the Leeds to Thirsk Railway to the city in the mid 19th Century. The canal linked the centre of Ripon with the River Ure near Bishop Monkton, a distance of only around two and a half miles from where boats used the river which was navigable all the way to York and beyond via a handful of cuts and locks. The canal has recently been restored and stands as the most northerly point of the English Canal Network.

**4.** *Retrace your steps back to the Bondgate Green Bridge where you turn right along the riverside path again to reach a footbridge above a weir adjacent to the Water Rat pub. Cross this footbridge and head straight on to quickly join Low St Agnesgate which you follow up then left at the junction along High St Agnesgate. Follow this straight on all the way to reach the main road again.*

The present-day road of **Low St Agnesgate** follows an ancient route between important crossings of the rivers Skell and Ure, although only a footbridge now spans the Skell. As you turn into **High St Agnesgate** there is a wonderful view of the imposing Cathedral, whilst on your left is an exquisite row of Victorian brick-built houses dating from 1863. This is the heart of the old city of Ripon, and the site of the original **Celtic monastery of St Cuthbert** - there are so many fine old buildings here that this was obviously the place to live centuries ago if you were a wealthy merchant or servant of the Church. Look out for **St Agnes Lodge** with its circular windows, a medieval manor house adapted and altered in the 17th Century although it still retains its cruck-framed design. The small building and parking area across the road was once the site of **Ripon Grammar School** which was established during the reign of Queen Mary in 1555; it moved to Bishopton in 1874. The next house along is the **Old Hall,** a superb red brick Georgian house dating from 1738 that stands on the site of a medieval building; Lewis Carroll stayed here during the 1850's. Further along the road are the ruins of **St Anne's Chapel Hospital,** one of the city's three ecclesiastical hospitals that was established in 1430. It is said that the ransom for the release of a Scottish king was paid on the altar of this chapel. The next house along is **Thorpe Prebend House,** one of the most important buildings in Ripon although sadly in a poor state of repair; renovation plans are in hand. A 'prebend' is an ecclesiastical estate that provided the church and its clergymen, especially canons, with revenue and the Thorpe Prebend can probably trace its history back to pre-Conquest days. This ancient house was rebuilt in 1609 and it is said that King James I and Mary Queen of Scots stayed here.

**5.** *At the main road turn right to quickly reach a roundabout where you follow the road up to the right (Bedern Bank) to reach the Cathedral. Turn left here along Kirkgate back into the Market Place.*

The striking 13th Century West Front of **Ripon Cathedral** dominates the city skyline, an architectural masterpiece of stone. The Cathedral is famed for its **Saxon Crypt,** a simple and thought-provoking chamber deep beneath the Nave and the oldest complete Saxon crypt in England. This is all that remains of the Saxon monastery founded in 672AD by St Wilfred above which towers the magnificent Norman Cathedral. St Cuthbert's Celtic monastery was situated just to the north of the present Cathedral and was founded in 660AD, however when St Wilfred became Abbot a few years later he adopted the Roman tradition of worship and many of the Celtic monks left. St Wilfred's Saxon monastery was destroyed during the 10th Century, however work began on a 'new' cathedral around 1154 taking centuries to complete. Inside there is a wealth of architecture to marvel at including the intricately carved choir stalls and misericords, the small seats monks used to rest against whilst standing during long services, carved in the 15th Century by the famous

Ripon School of Carvers. **Lewis Carroll** gained inspiration for his book 'Alice in Wonderland' from these carved misericords and the Crypt with its narrow passageways and hidden corners - perhaps the famous rabbit hole? The ornamental gardens to the north of the Cathedral were the site of the **Palace of the Archbishop of York.** Behind the high stone wall on the left is the **Old Courthouse,** a stone-built medieval building with a 'new' half-timbered house built onto it in 1613. This house was used as an ecclesiastical court in the Middle Ages as well as the city's prison and was still in use in Victorian times. To the right of the gardens is the **Old Deanery Hotel,** a 17th Century house that was originally the Dean's residence. The high stone that encloses this house and runs alongside the road is known as **Huby's Wall.** In the early 16th Century Marmaduke Huby, the Abbot of Fountains Abbey, planned to establish a group of monks at Ripon to help revive monastic life - this old boundary wall is all that remains. **Kirkgate** is one of the oldest streets in Ripon leading from the heart of the city to the West Front of the Cathedral. Half way down this street on the right is an old archway that was originally the entrance to the Archbishop of York's Palace and was later used by stagecoaches calling at the Unicorn Inn. Hidden away through the archway is a lovely row of four Georgian houses known as **Court Terrace.**

# Robin Hood's Bay

**TIME:** One & a half hours

**START:** This walk starts from the larger car park by the old Railway Station.

**TOILETS:** Main car park at the top of Bay Bank or the Old Lifeboat Station.

**CAFÉ:** Several to choose from including The Old Bakery, The Chapel and Bramblewick's.

**PUBS:** Choose from the Bay Hotel, Ye Dolphin Hotel or the Laurel Inn in the 'Old Town' or the Victoria Hotel 'Upbank'.

**PARKING:** Large car park off Station Road / Thorpe Road, also smaller car park at the top of Bay Bank.

**INFORMATION:** The Old Coastguard Station, Robin Hood's Bay: 01947 885900
Whitby Tourist Information Centre: 01947 602674

> *"Many of the cottages had secret passages that linked one house to another – it was said that illegal contraband could pass from the bottom to the top of the village without seeing daylight!"*

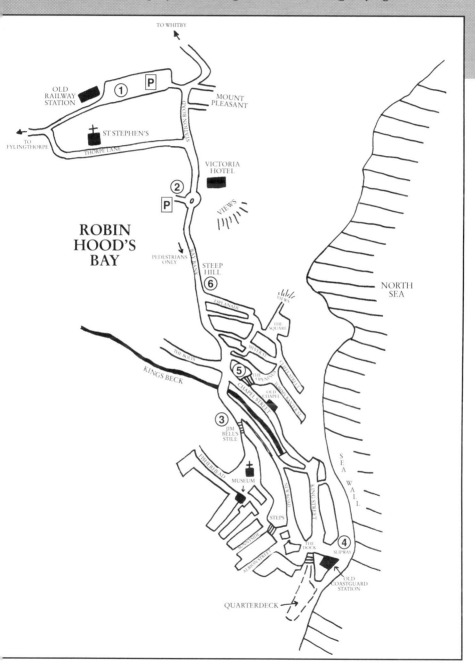

TO WHITBY

OLD RAILWAY STATION

① P

MOUNT PLEASANT

ST STEPHEN'S

TO FYLINGTHORPE

THORPE LANE

STATION ROAD

VICTORIA HOTEL

② P

VIEWS

ROBIN HOOD'S BAY

PEDESTRIANS ONLY

BAY BANK

STEEP HILL ⑥

ESPLANADE

VIEWS

THE SQUARE

NORTH SEA

THE BOLTS

SILVER ST

FISHER STREET

KINGS BECK

⑤ THE OPENINGS

OLD CHAPEL

MARINER'S RD

CHAPEL STREET

③ JIM BELL'S STILE

FISHERHEAD

MUSEUM

NEW ROAD

KING STREET

SEA WALL

STEPS

SUNNYSIDE

ALBION STREET

THE DOCK

④ SLIPWAY

OLD COASTGUARD STATION

QUARTERDECK

*1. From the main Car Park at the top of Station Road, walk through the parking area passing the former Railway Station on your right down to reach Thorpe Road. Turn left here, passing St Stephen's Church to the T-Junction with Station Road where you turn right down to the roundabout above the Old Town.*

Robin Hood's Bay, known locally as 'Bay Town' or simply 'Bay', is perhaps the prettiest of a string of picturesque fishing villages along the Yorkshire coast. A jumble of tiny cottages connected by a maze of passageways cling precariously to steep cliffs around the ravine of King's Beck for protection against the North Sea gales. There are several theories as to how this small town got its name. One story suggests that the famed outlaw fled here to escape capture and disguised himself as a fisherman, however, it seems unlikely that Robin Hood ever came here as the first mention of 'Robbyn Huddes Bay' was in the mid 16th Century, long after the exploits of Robin Hood in Sherwood Forest. There are two distinct parts to Robin Hood's Bay. The area on the shelf of land above the cliffs is known as **Upbank** and is the 'new' part of the town, which developed following the arrival of the railway in 1885. This coastal railway from Scarborough to Whitby was one of the most scenic in the country until it fell victim to Dr Beeching's axe in 1965. **St Stephens Church** has served the Parish of Fylingdales since it was built in 1870 replacing the original 12th Century St Stephen's Church half a mile to the north that fell out of use due to its isolated location. The 'new' church is noted for its tall bell tower, stained glass windows, interesting memorials and the Norman font from the 'original' church. We soon reach the roundabout at the top of Bay Bank with views of the sweeping bay across the rooftops of the 'Old Town'. Note the memorial on the right to the bravery of the local people who were unable to launch Bay's smaller lifeboat during a terrible storm in January 1881 and so dragged the Whitby lifeboat for six miles through snow drifts and saved the crew of the brig 'Visitor'.

*2. Walk down Bay Bank and follow it as it twists down to reach the bridge over King's Beck. Carry on for a short distance then follow Jim Bell's Stile (steps) up to the right after Beckfield House.*

**Bay Bank** leads steeply down into the heart of the Old Town with its 'Toy Town' appearance of old fishermen's cottages crammed into every available space connected by a maze of passages. We soon pass the **Laurel Inn**, once the haunt of smugglers - there is said to be a secret tunnel leading from this pub to King's Beck. During the 18th Century, high taxes on imported luxury goods such as rum and tobacco, coupled with Bay's isolated location, meant that smuggling became a lucrative occupation - it soon became the 'Smuggling Capital of the North' with almost everyone involved on a very organised basis. Many of the cottages had secret passages that linked one house to another - it was said that illegal contraband could pass from the bottom to the top of the village without seeing daylight! Just before the bridge is a lane known as **The Bolts,** so called as this provided a quick means of escape when the Excise Officers and Press Gang were in town.

**3.** *Walk up along Jim Bell's Stile then pass to the right of the Congregational Church to reach the row of cottages at Fisherhead. Turn left here passing the old Coroners Court, then at the end of the houses turn right then immediately left down a flight of steps (Tyson's Steps). Follow these down bearing to the left to join New Road again. Turn right here to quickly reach The Dock and the slipway onto the beach.*

**Jim Bell's Stile** leads up to a maze of cottages surrounding the **Congregational Church** which was built in 1840 and is still in use as a United Reformed Church; note the **whalebones** in the garden of a cottage in front of the church. This area is known as **Fisherhead**, as fishing boats were dragged up from the beach onto the grassy cliffs beyond here. The sea once claimed so many lives that a **Coroner's Court and Mortuary** was built in the row of cottages known as Fisherhead; this now houses a small museum. As you turn right along New Road again, the four-storey white-washed house on the left known as **'Fisherman's Cottage'** and dated 1680 was once the Fisherman's Arms, a favourite haunt of the town's smugglers. At the foot of New Road is **The Dock**, a small area with stacks of lobster pots and one or two fishing boats. During winter storms, waves crash up this slipway sending foaming water across The Dock; it is said that the bowsprit of a sailing ship crashed through a window of the **Bay Hotel** during a bad storm. By the mid 19th Century Robin Hood's Bay had become the most important fishing village along the Yorkshire coast with over 130 fishermen living in the town from where they set out in their traditional flat bottomed fishing boats known as 'cobles'. The town's heyday was during the 18th and 19th Centuries when fishing, shipping and smuggling was at its height, however fishing declined during the early 20th Century as the cramped facilities at Bay could not accommodate the new larger ships. The old **Lifeboat Station,** now used as a shelter with a bench, closed in 1931 after fifty years service - the town is now served by the Whitby Lifeboat. The last house on the right before the North Sea is the **Old Coastguard Station,** which has recently been rebuilt by The National Trust to regain its Victorian appearance. It began as a lookout for ships in distress and smugglers in the early 19th Century, but was later used as a Marine Laboratory by the University of Leeds and then a Management Training Centre until the National Trust bought it in 1998. This now houses a fascinating Visitor Centre that brings the Yorkshire coastline to life. The stretch of coast has been designated a Heritage Coast, whilst the bay itself has been classified as a Site of Special Scientific Interest and a Sensitive Marine Area due to its geology and wildlife. At low tide huge crescent shaped ridges of rock are revealed, formed as the sea erodes soft shale in between harder limestone. This area is the haunt of geologists and fossil collectors, but an eye must be kept on the tide. **King's Beck** tumbles into the North Sea through The Tunnel, once the main way into the town for contraband - blocked up secret passageways can still be seen within its dark depths.

John A. Ives
'01

**4.** *At The Dock follow the road round to the left climbing up along King Street, at the top of which turn left along Chapel Street. Follow this lane as it bends round to the right then on above King's Beck passing the old Chapel on your right. Just before the steps down onto New Road turn right up the steps "The Openings leading to The Square".*

**King Street** was once the main road into the town, however a severe storm during the 1780's washed away much of the street and several cottages. This stretch of coastline is notorious for its storms as over the centuries more than 200 cottages have disappeared into the sea. A large sea wall was built during the 1970's to protect the Old Town and more recently another sea wall has been constructed as well as large piles of huge boulders to protect the surrounding cliffs. However, it is only a matter of time as the sea is relentlessly eating away at the soft cliffs at a rate of around five metres every 100 years. Further along King Street is the house where novelist **Leo Walmsley** lived from 1894 until 1913. He wrote his most famous books during the 1930's about a fictional fishing village called Bramblewick (based upon Robin Hood's Bay) and the hard life of the Yorkshire fisherman. Further along the street is the very old stone-built **York House,** to the side of which is a passage that leads to the sea wall with wonderful views across the bay. **Chapel Street** became the main road into the town for a while after King Street disappeared, although it must have been a tight squeeze as the houses are set close together. We soon pass the old **Wesleyan Chapel,** which was built in 1779 and served as a Methodist Chapel until 1936; it is now a café, bookshop and craftshop.

**5.** *Walk up the steps along The Openings to quickly reach a 'crossroads' of paths at the palm tree. Head straight on along the left-hand fork (steps and handrail) and follow this up to reach The Square. Follow the passageway round to the left passing The Square on your right, then head round to the right at the top of Darnhill Steps (ignore steps), then left along Esplanade to reach Bay Bank again.*

**The Openings** leads into the 'heart' of the Old Town from where a maze of passageways beckon you to explore. The much-photographed view up towards Sunny Place, complete with a small palm tree, perhaps typifies the charm of Robin Hood's Bay. A cobbled passageway leads up past **Cliffe Street,** which once connected with King Street, into **The Square.** As the prosperity of the town grew, larger houses were built higher up the cliff - this square is the oldest affluent part of the town where many professional people once lived. Buildings of note include the **Mariners Tavern** that dates from 1668, a tiny pub that closed generations ago complete with a fire mark of the County Insurance Co. This is a reminder of the days before the Fire Brigade when individual householders bought protection from fire - if you did not have a fire mark, then the insurance company's private fire brigade would not come to your rescue! **Wesley Cottage** is named after John Wesley who preached in The Square on several occasions during the late 18th Century. **Bloomswell Terrace** and the **Esplanade** are two fine rows of three-storey brick-built Victorian houses with small gardens.

**6.** *Turn right back up Bay Bank to the roundabout then head straight on along Station Road back to the Car Park and the start.*

The large houses and hotels at the top of the bank date from the late 19th Century following the arrival of the railway, which brought tourists to this picturesque seaside resort. The **Victoria Hotel** of 1897 stands proudly on the edge of the cliffs with wonderful views across the bay, whilst further along Station Road is an area known as **Mount Pleasant** with two streets of large Victorian villas that were built for the many wealthy ship-owners of Robin Hood's Bay, whose fortunes were reputedly made from the proceeds of smuggling.

# Scarborough

**TIME:** Three hours

**START:** Scarborough Castle

**TOILETS:** Several located around the Town Centre and along Foreshore Road.

**CAFÉ:** Numerous teashops throughout the town.

**PUBS:** Plenty of choice: try the Hole in the Wall on Vernon Road, the Lord Rosebery on Westborough or the Scarborough Arms on North Terrace.

**PARKING:** There are several large car parks around the main Town Centre (Westborough).

**INFORMATION:** Scarborough Tourist Information Centre: 01723 373333

*"With a history stretching back to the early 17th Century, Scarborough is England's oldest seaside resort. In 1626 Mrs Farrer, a wealthy local lady, 'discovered' a mineral spring bubbling up from beneath the South Cliffs and claimed it to be of medicinal benefit partly due to its foul taste!"*

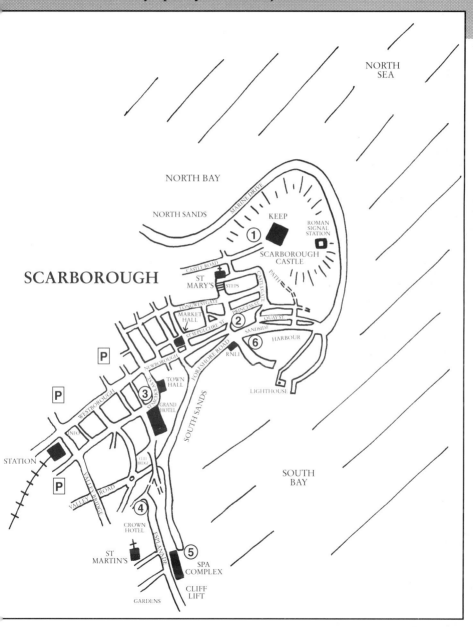

1. *From Scarborough Castle walk down along Castle Road and then through the churchyard to reach St Mary's Church. From the south doorway of the Church, take the left-hand fork in the path that leads through an archway then steeply down Church Stairs Street. Follow this street straight on down to reach Princess Street and Princess Square.*

Scarborough is dominated by its **Castle,** which stands sentinel above the town on a rocky headland between the North and South Bays. This strategic promontory has been used throughout the ages with evidence of settlement during the Bronze Age, the remains of a Roman Signal Station and a 10th Century chapel built by Viking invaders, who also established the town of Scarborough along what is now Quay Street. Indeed, the town is named after a Viking called Thorgils Skardi - this was the stronghold (or 'borough') of Skardi. The first castle was built here following the Norman Conquest when William le Gros was made Earl of York and given land by King Stephen in 1138. However, when Henry II came to the throne in 1154 he demanded the return of all the Royal castles, including Scarborough. The King embarked on a major rebuilding programme, which included the massive stone Keep. Building works continued throughout the 13th Century and soon Scarborough became one of the most important Royal castles in England; the last King to stay here was Richard III in 1484. The Castle was put to the test during the Civil War as this was a Royalist stronghold in a predominantly Parliamentarian region. Following the defeat of the Royalists at the Battle of Marston Moor in 1644 the Parliamentarians turned their attention to Scarborough and lay siege to the Castle bombarding it for five months, eventually forcing the Royalists to surrender; the west wall of the Keep collapsed during this siege. I recommend a tour of the Castle to see the impressive 14th Century Barbican, 12th Century Keep, Roman Signal Station and wonderful views across the town. **Anne Brontë** died on a visit to Scarborough in May 1849 whilst suffering from tuberculosis and lies buried in St Mary's churchyard, although her gravestone is incorrect as she was actually 29 years old when she died. **St Mary's Church** dates from the late 12th Century, however it was extended considerably in the 13th to 15th Centuries; note the 14th Century chapels off the South Aisle with their unusual stone vaulted ceilings. During the Civil War St Mary's was used by the Parliamentarians as a base to attack the Royalist Castle and consequently suffered considerable damage from cannon fire; the ruins of the Chancel can still be seen in the churchyard. The ancient thoroughfare of **Church Stairs Street** leads down into the heart of the Old Town. It was here that the wealthy merchants and sea captains built their homes during the 18th and 19th Centuries above the cramped fishing village near the Harbour; the streets around here are lined with many elegant Georgian town houses. Just off **Princess Square** is the **Butter Cross,** a slender stone market cross that once acted to remind traders to deal fairly in the many street markets that flourished around here in medieval times. It is also the last remaining link with the once famous Scarborough Fair.

**2.** *Turn right through Princess Square and head straight on along St Sepulchre Street up to reach the Market Hall. Follow the flagged path to the left of the Market Hall to quickly reach St Helen's Square in front of its main entrance. Turn left here down to reach a road junction then turn right up along Newborough until you reach the next junction where you turn left along St Nicholas Street down to reach the Town Hall.*

Situated along **St Sepulchre Street** is the "**Hospital of Trinity House**", founded in 1602 by the 'Society of Ship Owners and Master Mariners' to provide almshouses for old or disabled merchant seamen. This institution, one of only four in the country, became wealthy and powerful during the 18th and 19th Centuries and controlled the business of the port from this building. Trinity House was rebuilt in 1832 and again in 1872 and is still used as a home for retired seamen. The imposing **Market Hall** was built in 1853 to replace the overcrowded street markets that had been held in this area since medieval times. **St Nicholas Street** leads off the main shopping area and boasts many fine buildings including Barclays Bank, an ornate Victorian building that was originally the home of local bankers Bell & Woodall. **Scarborough Town Hall** was originally built as a private house (St Nicholas House) in the 1840's for John Woodall, who had made his fortune from banking. The house was sold to the Corporation in 1898 and subsequently became the Town Hall. Across the road from here is the **Royal Hotel,** which stands on the site of the fashionable Long Room where elegant balls were held during the 18th Century for the wealthy visitors to the Spa. The Long Room was gradually extended during the 19th Century until it developed into the present-day Royal Hotel, where many famous guests have stayed including Sir Winston Churchill.

**3.** *Continue along St Nicholas Street following it round to the right then take the turning to the left along St Nicholas Cliff passing in front of the Grand Hotel. Head straight on across Cliff Bridge after which the path divides - follow the right-hand branch that leads up a flight of steps to reach the Esplanade.*

The **Grand Hotel** really is grand in every sense and dominates the South Bay skyline, its four towers rising up above an incredibly ornate six-storey building. The need for a large hotel grew following the arrival of the railway in 1845, which brought more and more wealthy visitors to this flourishing Spa town and seaside resort. The hotel was designed by Cuthbert Broderick, who also designed Leeds Town Hall, and when it opened in 1867 was the largest hotel in Europe. **Cliff Bridge,** also known as the Spa Footbridge, opened in 1827 as a toll bridge to allow easier access to the Spa from the town centre; tolls were abolished in 1951. From the bridge you can see the **Rotunda Museum** down to the right, built in 1829 as the first museum where display determined the design of the building. It originally housed a display of geological rock formations and fossils and has since developed into a local history museum.

**4.** *Walk straight on along the Esplanade and follow this down until it opens out with the Esplanade Gardens and Prince of Wales Terrace to your right. Take either the Cliff Lift ('Tramway to Spa Complex and Beach') or one of the paths that lead down to reach the Spa Complex on the sea-front.*

The construction of the Cliff Bridge opened up the **South Cliff** for development and this area soon became the fashionable place for wealthy Victorians to live. **The Esplanade** boasts some of Scarborough's finest Victorian buildings, with a superb sweeping terrace of cream-coloured villas and hotels built during the 1840's, at the centre of which is the magnificent **Crown Hotel** with its Doric columns supporting a large portico. Magnificent buildings such as this helped give rise to the claim that Scarborough was the 'Brighton of the North'. A short detour along St Martin's Avenue brings you to the **Parish Church of St Martin-on-the-Hill,** built in the 1860's to serve the affluent South Cliff area. The church is famous for its wealth of stained glass, paintings and decorations made by the Pre-Raphaelite artists of the 19th Century, probably the best collection of Victorian religious art anywhere. The short but steep journey on the **Cliff Lift** to the Spa Complex is a memorable experience. Built in 1875, this was the first cliff railway in England.

*5. Turn left passing in front of The Spa Complex heading back towards the town with South Sands to your right. The road soon joins the main Foreshore Road, which you follow straight on to reach the Harbour.*

With a history stretching back to the early 17th Century, Scarborough is England's oldest seaside resort. In 1626 Mrs Farrer, a wealthy local lady, 'discovered' a mineral spring bubbling up from beneath the South Cliffs and claimed it to be of medicinal benefit partly due to its foul taste! News quickly spread and before long many doctors were prescribing it for almost every ailment. Scarborough soon developed into a fashionable resort, however facilities remained fairly basic until the early 19th Century. In 1839 a stone 'Gothic Saloon' was constructed above the spring, which heralded the development of the Spa as an entertainment centre. This was enlarged in 1847 and again in 1858 when a Concert Hall was built and the surrounding gardens landscaped, however these buildings were gutted by fire in 1876. The present **Spa Complex,** including the Grand Hall and Spa Theatre, dates from the rebuilding of 1880. In its heyday Scarborough became a flourishing seaside health resort - the 'Queen of Watering Places' for wealthy Victorians. Although the Pump Room closed in 1939, the Spa Complex remains a popular entertainment and conference centre. A pleasant stroll alongside the South Sands takes you back into the heart of the town with **South Bay** sweeping gracefully round towards the Castle. At the top of the beach is the **Lifeboat Station,** one of the oldest in the British Isles, founded in 1801.

*6. Continue heading up along what is now Sandside with the Harbour to your right, then as you approach the end of the Harbour turn left down the lane to the side of the Lancaster pub to reach Quay Street. Take the steps directly ahead (Dog & Duck Lane) at the top of which turn left along Burr Bank and follow this down to join Castlegate at a bend in the road. Turn right and head steeply back up bending round to the left along Paradise then round to the right along Church Lane to the Castle.*

The historic harbour area has served as a port since Viking times, however it was not until 1252 that a purpose-built timber and stone harbour was constructed following a charter granted by Henry III. The **Harbour** was enlarged again in the 16th and 18th Centuries when it became one of the busiest ports in England. The **West Pier,** with its harbour buildings and fish market, was rebuilt in 1820 to form a new entrance to the inner harbour. The **North Wharf,** where many of the fishing boats are moored, was rebuilt in 1926 at the zenith of the herring trade. Across the Harbour is Vincent's Pier that dates from 1752 with its famous Lighthouse of 1804, although this was badly damaged by German Naval bombardment in 1914 and subsequently rebuilt. Scarborough's third pier, known as the East or **Outer Pier,** was constructed in the early 19th Century. This is still a thriving fishing port with traditional 'cobles' and larger keel boats landing their catches of crab, lobster, haddock, whiting and plaice. The Harbour was also once a major centre for shipbuilding during the 17th and 18th Centuries, however by the late 19th Century this industry had died out. Across the road from the Harbour is the historic **King Richard III House,** which dates back to the mid 14th Century and is where Richard Plantagenet, later Richard III, reputedly stayed in the 15th Century when he held the post of Lord High Admiral. An alleyway leads down the side of the Lancaster pub to reach **Quay Street** in the historic heart of Scarborough. This was the site of the original Viking settlement and later served as the main street in medieval times. A number of ancient half-timbered houses remain including the **Three Mariners,** a cruck-framed house that dates back to the 14th Century. Reputedly the oldest pub in the town, this was a favourite watering hole for smugglers 300 years ago; it is now a private house. Sadly, many houses have disappeared over the years - the cobbled and paved road indicates the original course and width of Quay Street. If you follow Quay Street to the left it soon joins a back alleyway known as **The Bolts** that runs behind the sea-front shops to join Eastborough adjacent to the West Pier, a hidden reminder of medieval Scarborough.

# Settle

**TIME:** Two hours

**START:** Settle Market Place.

**TOILETS:** Car parks off Church Street and Station Road.

**CAFÉ:** Several to choose from; try Ye Olde Naked Man in the Market Place or Sidwells along Cheapside.

**PUBS:** The Golden Lion Inn along Duke Street, Royal Oak Hotel in the Market Place or The Talbot Inn along High Street.

**PARKING:** Whitefriars Car Park off Church Street and Ashfield Car Park off Station Road.

**INFORMATION:** Settle Tourist Information Centre: 01729 825192

**MARKET DAY:** Tuesday

*"Facing across the Market Place towards The Shambles is a former inn that now serves as Ye Olde Naked Man Café, on the outside of which is the figure of a naked man with a conveniently placed date of 1663."*

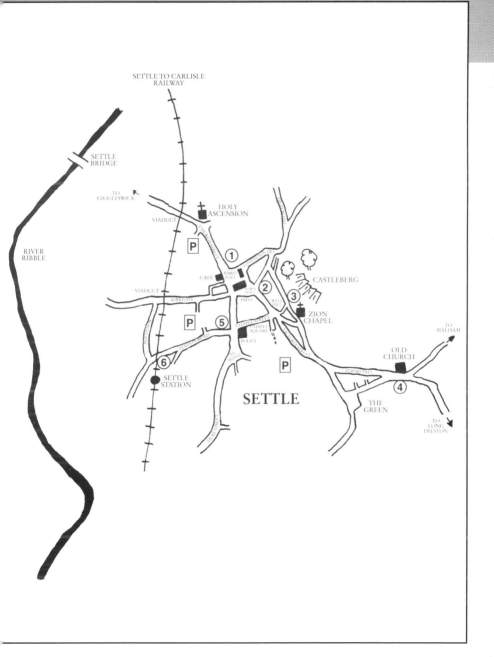

1. *From the Market Place head to the left of The Shambles and up along Constitution Hill then at the road junction with the Old Brewhouse on the corner turn right down along Castle Hill. Where this road divides follow the cobbled lane straight on down to reach the High Street.*

Settle is a bustling market town set amongst the rolling limestone hills of Ribblesdale in the Craven district of the Yorkshire Dales. During the 17th Century the town prospered as traffic increased along the old packhorse routes through the hills. Wealthy farmers and traders rebuilt their homes in stone, indeed one of the delights of the town is its many 17th Century cottages. In the 18th Century the Keighley to Kendal Turnpike came through Settle which heralded a new era of coaching inns, Georgian mansion houses and more organised industry including cotton mills along the River Ribble. But perhaps the town is most famous as the starting point of the Settle to Carlisle Railway, one of the most scenic railway journeys in the world. There has been a weekly market at Settle since King Henry III granted the town a Market Charter in 1249. A slender stone shaft above a Victorian drinking fountain stands at the heart of the **Market Place,** built in 1863 to replace the old Market Cross. Overlooking this area is **The Shambles,** a wonderful three-storey building with arcades around the ground floor, which dates back to the 17th Century when it was originally just an open market and later became the butchers' market - 'shambles' is the old word for butchers' shops. The arches and first floor buildings were added in the 18th Century and then a further storey was built during the 19th Century. Across to the right is the **Town Hall,** a grand Victorian Gothic building of 1832 that stands on the site of the old Toll Booth. Behind the Town Hall is a small bank building that was originally the home of the **Craven Savings Bank,** founded in the early 19th Century. Benjamin Waugh was born in a cottage on this site in 1839 and later founded the Society for the Prevention of Cruelty to Children. A short distance along Duke Street is the **Golden Lion Inn,** a wonderful old coaching inn with a large inglenook fireplace and sweeping staircase. This inn dates back to 1640 and was originally situated along Cheapside but moved to Duke Street in the mid 18th Century when the Turnpike came through the town. Facing across the Market Place towards The Shambles is a former inn that now serves as **Ye Olde Naked Man Café,** on the outside of which is the figure of a naked man with a conveniently placed date of 1663. To the left of The Shambles is a fine three-storey Georgian house, now the **NatWest Bank,** that was once the home of Dr Buck whose friend, Sir Edward Elgar, regularly came to stay. **Constitution Hill** leads up from the Market Place to join the old coach road to Langcliffe, known as the High Road. Note Hillside Cottage on your left with its fine carved doorway dated 1694. On the corner of **Castle Hill** and **Castleberg Lane** is an old Victorian warehouse still with its first floor loading bay hoist and fading sign for 'Danex' on the wall. This was once a farm supplies and merchants warehouse owned by the Thornber family that has since been converted into houses. A short detour up to your left along **Castleberg Lane** brings you to the working **blacksmith's shop** of D & R Clements, whose high quality decorative work and sculptures are very much in demand. The present owners took over about ten years ago from Alf Limmer, who had been a blacksmith here for over 50 years - there has been a smithy on this site since the 19th Century.

2. *Turn left along the High Street and follow this road down to the crossroads with Chapel Square ahead of you. Turn left along Victoria Street then immediately before The Folly turn left along a narrow lane (Well Hill) and follow this up passing the water troughs then up Well Hill Steps onto Castleberg Lane.*

**The Talbot Inn** dates back to the coaching era and still retains its coaching arch with old stabling and cottages behind. **Chapel Square** takes its name from an 18th Century

Wesleyan Chapel that once stood nearby. In the late 18th Century plans were drawn up to build a branch canal to Settle from the Leeds and Liverpool Canal with a canal basin beyond Chapel Square; now the only reminder of this ambitious plan is in the name of Liverpool House. Situated along Victoria Street is **The Folly**, Settle's most famous building. This wonderful rambling building was built in 1675, although some say 1679, for Richard Preston who had made his money through a leather tanning business - it was originally known as Tanner Hall. The house was subsequently bought in 1703 by Margaret Dawson of Langcliffe Hall, but a few years later the family moved out and it remained empty for many years, although the Dawson family continued to own it for over 250 years. It was during this long period of neglect that the house gained the name of The Folly. The house was restored in the 1950's and there are plans to convert part of it into the Museum of North Craven Life. A narrow lane leads up to the left of The Folly along **Well Hill**, which takes its name from the small spring and three old drinking troughs situated half way up. These were once used by both the people of the town and their animals for drinking water! Paths lead up from Castleberg Lane to the vantage point of **Castleberg**, a large limestone crag surmounted by a flag pole from where there are magnificent views across the town. Trees, gardens and paths were laid out in the 19th Century as a pleasant walkway up to the crag. Amazingly, this outcrop of rock was once used by the townsfolk as a gigantic sundial.

**3.** *Turn right along Castleberg Lane passing the Zion Chapel and Settle Primary School (ignore the lane down to your right by the stone milepost) to join Victoria Street. Head straight on along this road then where it opens out slightly with Commercial Street off to the right continue along the main road (Albert Hill) up to the left, with the signpost to 'Kirkby Malham, Airton'. Climb up this lane until you come to the road junction on the very edge of the town with the old Catholic Church on your left.*
You soon come to the simple **Independent Chapel** of 1816, still in use today as a Zion Congregational Church. This chapel looks out across a small triangular 'green' with an amazing building to your right known as the **Sutcliffe Buildings**. This ingenious house is actually a 'double' building set on a steep hill with four storey houses to the rear and three-storey houses to the front. Look out for the old **stone milepost** set into the wall with miles to "London 236, Kirkby Lonsdale 17, Hawes 26, Skipton 16, Lancaster 26". In the days before the Turnpike, **Victoria Street** was the main road into Settle with busy routes heading over the hills to Malham and Long Preston. The old road then continued through the Market Place and down along Kirkgate towards Giggleswick. Where Victoria Street opens out slightly near the turning along Commercial Street is a small **Primitive Methodist Chapel** of 1841 set back from the road, now converted into a house. **Albert Hill** boasts a variety of houses stretching

back over 300 years including Twistleton's Yard, a cobbled yard overlooked by Victorian cottages. You soon reach the road junction on the edge of the town with moorland roads stretching away into the distance. On your left is the old **Catholic Church,** built in the 1860's in typical Victorian Gothic design - perhaps its isolated location was compensated by its rather pious position above the town. It was replaced by a new Catholic Church off Church Street and has since been converted into houses.

**4.** *At the road junction turn to the right back on yourself along Greenhead Lane. Follow this down until it opens out onto The Green. Walk straight on, passing The Green on your left, and out along Commercial Street to the right. Follow Commercial Street down to quickly join Victoria Street again and head straight on bearing left at the fork in the road down along the cobbled lane (still Victoria Street) passing The Folly then round to the left (now Chapel Street) to reach the T-junction with Duke Street.*

**Greenhead Lane** leads steeply down to reach **The Green,** a delightful area hidden away from the bustle of the town with a picturesque 'green' complete with a red 'phone box and a large tree planted to commemorate Queen Victoria's Diamond Jubilee. This area is known as Upper Settle and was originally a small farming community set above the old market town. Across The Green down to the left is a farmhouse of immense character built in 1682. In the late 18th Century this was used as a tannery, for Settle was once famous for its leather with traders travelling from far and wide to buy leather products. As you walk down along Victoria Street you pass a number of old buildings including the three-storey **Primrose Cottage** with the remains of a barn entrance, and also Primrose House with its datestone of 1664 and initials of the Wildman family who originally built this old farmhouse. On the corner of Chapel Street and Duke Street is the rather grand **Police Station,** formerly a mansion house known as Cragdale that was built in the early 19th Century for John Peart, a local lawyer and partner in the Craven Bank. The large Georgian house opposite was originally known as **Ashfield House** (now the Settle Social Club) and was built for William Birkbeck who, along with William Alcock and John Peart, founded the Craven Bank in 1791, famous for its banknotes with a picture of a large cow on them! The bank later became part of Barclays. Perhaps the most famous family member was **George Birkbeck** (1776 - 1841) who founded the Mechanics Institute in the early 19th Century, a once flourishing institution that provided free education for the working classes.

**5.** *Turn left along Duke Street then take the first turning to the right along Station Road and follow this down to reach Settle Station.*

Before the Keighley to Kendal Turnpike came through the town, **Duke Street** was just a rough track known as Duck Lane that led from the Market Place to the duck pond and some outlying farms beyond the **Triangle,** as the small 'square' area beyond the turning for Station Road is known. Of particular note is **Nelson's Footwear Shop** with its Art Décor façade. Five successive generations of the Nelson family have been making shoes here since 1847. Situated along **Station Road** is the **Old Courthouse,** now the home of Settle Amateur Operatic Society, after which is the old police station with its prominent stone lintels. You soon come down to **Settle Station.** The Midland Railway Co. completed the Settle to Carlisle Railway in 1876 as they needed a route to Scotland to compete with the rival coastal lines. It stands today as one of the great feats of Victorian engineering with twenty major viaducts and fourteen tunnels along the 72 miles of track that rises to a height of 1,169-ft at Aisgill Summit - and all built using little more than muscle power. Settle Station has been restored to its former glory and is a good example of Midland Railway's 'Derby Gothic' architecture. The railway passes through the town across a series of viaducts and an embankment.

**6.** *Continue along Station Road beneath the railway bridge then turn right along Bond Lane and follow this down to the next T-junction. Turn right here up along Kirkgate, beneath the railway viaduct then turn left along a cobbled yard (Bishopdale Court) opposite Dugdales Store and follow this back up into the Market Place.*
**Kirkgate** was the main route through the town in pre-Turnpike days and once led to the ancient Parish Church of St Alkelda at Giggleswick. Just after the railway viaduct is the **Friends Meeting House,** which has been in constant use by Quakers since 1678. This is one of the earliest Meeting Houses in the country, founded some eleven years before the Toleration Act of 1689 that allowed dissenting Protestants (Nonconformists) the freedom of worship. Across the road is **Victoria Hall,** built in 1853 as a Music Hall and still used for concerts and events. An indoor market is also held here every Tuesday. Just up from here is **Spread Eagle House,** a fine Georgian house that was formerly a coaching inn. Thomas Proctor was born here in 1753, a noted painter, sculptor and member of the Royal Academy. **Dugdales** is a traditional ironmongers and hardware shop that has served the needs of the town since 1906. To its right hidden down an alleyway is **Weavers Cottage,** with an ornate doorway dated '1664'. In the 17th and 18th Centuries weaving was a thriving cottage industry with several weavers living along Kirkgate. **Bishopdale Court** leads off Kirkgate, a lovely cobbled yard and one of the oldest in the town, with the 17th Century Bishopdale House situated along the narrowest part of the yard.

# Skipton

**TIME:** Three hours

**START:** Skipton Castle

**TOILETS:** Situated in either the Coach Street car park or the Town Hall car park.

**CAFÉ:** Countless cafés to choose from: try High Street Tea Rooms near the Town Hall, the Coffee Mill along Otley Street or Waterside Cottage Tea Rooms along Coach Street.

**PUBS:** Numerous pubs; try the Black Horse along the High Street, the Woolly Sheep Inn along Sheep Street, the Narrow Boat along Victoria Street or The Castle along Mill Bridge.

**PARKING:** Large car parks off Water Street or behind the Town Hall off Rectory Lane.

**INFORMATION:** Skipton Tourist Information Centre: 01756 792809

**MARKET DAYS:** Monday, Wednesday, Friday and Saturday.

> *"However, there is another side to this town. In the 1770's a canal was built connecting Skipton with Leeds and soon large cotton mills and rows of terraced houses were built beside this waterway, a fascinating legacy of the Industrial Revolution."*

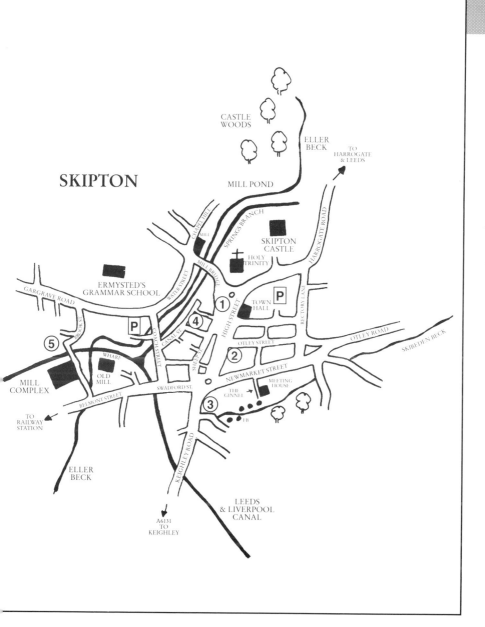

SKIPTON

CASTLE WOODS

ELLER BECK

TO HARROGATE & LEEDS

MILL POND

SPRINGS BRANCH

CHAPEL HILL

MILL

MILL BRIDGE

SKIPTON CASTLE

HOLY TRINITY

HARROGATE ROAD

ERMYSTED'S GRAMMAR SCHOOL

GARGRAVE ROAD

WATER STREET

BROOK ST

COACH STREET

CANAL ST

HIGH STREET

TOWN HALL

P

RECTORY LANE

OTLEY STREET

OTLEY ROAD

SKIBEDEN BECK

SHEEP ST

① ④ ② ③ ⑤

P

WHARF

OLD MILL

MILL COMPLEX

NEWMARKET STREET

MEETING HOUSE

SWADFORD ST

BELMONT STREET

THE GINNEL

FB

TO RAILWAY STATION

ELLER BECK

KEIGHLEY ROAD

A6131 TO KEIGHLEY

LEEDS & LIVERPOOL CANAL

**1.** *From Holy Trinity Church and Skipton Castle, walk down through the High Street then, where the wide market place narrows, turn left along Otley Street.*

Skipton was first settled by Anglo-Saxon sheep farmers in the 7th Century, indeed the name of the town literally means 'sheep town'. It remained a small farming community until the years following the Norman Conquest when a castle was built and the town quickly grew as a trading centre, particularly for livestock and woollen products from the Craven District of the southern Yorkshire Dales. However, there is another side to this town. In the 1770's a canal was built connecting Skipton with Leeds and soon large cotton mills and rows of terraced houses were built beside this waterway, a fascinating legacy of the Industrial Revolution. **Holy Trinity Church** dominates the town, its sturdy tower rising above the High Street. The Church was founded alongside the Norman castle in the 11th Century, although the present building dates mainly from the early 14th Century. The church boasts a wealth of treasures such as a magnificent oak roof with unusual carved bosses including the pagan symbol of a 'Green Man', a fine 16th Century Chancel Screen, the remains of an Anchorite Cell that dates from the Middle Ages and the ornate tomb of George Clifford, third Earl of Cumberland, who died in 1605. **Skipton Castle** was first established in the 11th Century when Robert de Romille, a Norman baron, built a castle on the crags above Eller Beck. Edward II granted the Castle to Robert Clifford in 1310, who became the first Lord Clifford of Skipton and subsequently rebuilt the Castle as a strong stone fortress - it remained the family's principal seat until the death of Lady Anne Clifford in 1676. During the Civil War Parliamentarian forces laid siege to the Castle, however it took three years before the Royalist forces finally surrendered. The Castle was then partially destroyed under Cromwell's orders, though Lady Anne Clifford was granted permission to rebuild a less defensive castle only a few years later - much of what you see today dates from this rebuilding during the 1650's. Today, Skipton Castle stands as one of the best preserved medieval castles in the country and is still fully roofed. From the gatehouse with its double round towers above which is an inscription 'Desormais' ('henceforth'), there is a wonderful view of the Keep with its imposing round towers. A fascinating leaflet will guide you around the many well-preserved rooms, at the heart of which is the attractive Conduit Court with its ancient yew tree, planted by Lady Anne Clifford in 1659. Descendants of the Clifford family owned the Castle until the 1950's when it was bought by a local family, who still live in the Tudor Wing. The feudal title of the Lord of the Honour of Skipton ('honour' was an area of land) has been passed down through the centuries along with the ownership of the Castle, with jurisdiction over areas such as Skipton Woods and the market. The poignant **War Memorial,** with its angel and kneeling soldier, looks down along the **High Street** where a bustling street market takes over the cobbled verges four days a week. Skipton was granted its Market Charter in 1204 by King John and is one of the oldest market towns in Yorkshire. Until 1906 the High

Street was also used as the cattle market, however the smell became too much for local people and it was moved to a site behind the Town Hall, now used as a car park, before moving to the Auction Mart on the outskirts of the town. Standing proudly near the top of the High Street is the **Town Hall** of 1862, with its fine two-storey portico supported by Doric columns. The Town Hall houses council offices, a large concert hall and the **Craven Museum,** a fascinating collection of artefacts from the local area including Bronze Age swords, Roman relics and items from the lead mining days. Across from here is the **Black Horse,** an ancient hostelry that was originally known as the King's Head until the 1720's and once housed the Royal Mews of King Richard III when he held the title of Lord of the Honour of Skipton in the 15th Century; the pub was rebuilt in 1676. It is said that during the Civil War Parliamentarian soldiers were served poisoned ale by the landlord who was a Royalist supporter. Further down along the High Street is the **Yorkshire Bank** that stands on the site of the old Bay Horse Inn, in front of which bulls were once tethered for baiting. A few doors down from the turning along Otley Street is **Barclays Bank** outside which once stood the stocks and a large Market Cross crowned by a bell that was rung to signal the start and end of market trading. These were removed in about 1840 and the ancient bell now hangs inside **Craven Court Shopping Centre.** This Shopping Centre is housed in an old yard that has been tastefully converted and retains many lovely old buildings beneath a glass roof. One of the shops was formerly a pub known as the Hole-in-the-wall, behind which a theatre company used to stage performances; Edmund Kean and Harriet Mellon performed here in 1807.

2. *Follow Otley Street all the way down to reach the junction with Rectory Lane, where you turn right to quickly join Newmarket Street (main road). Turn right along Newmarket Street passing St Andrews Church on your right then turn left along an alleyway known as The Ginnel opposite the turning for Court Lane / Providence Place. Follow this down to reach a stream, where you turn right along the riverside path, over a footbridge and on to join a lane which you follow down to the right to reach the main Keighley Road.*

**Otley Street** is a quiet cobbled side street, home to a variety of old fashioned shops including **Drake and Macefield** Butchers' shop, a family run business since 1898, renowned for their award-winning pies. You soon reach **Skipton County Court**, a fine stone-built courthouse that dates back to 1847 with a rather grand Royal Coat of Arms above the door. **Kipling House** (No. 24 Otley Street) was once the home of Rudyard Kipling's grandfather, Rev Joseph Kipling, who was a Wesleyan Minister in the town. Rudyard came to stay here as a boy during the 1840's and 50's. **St Andrews Church** and associated Church Hall can be found along Newmarket Street and are today used as a Methodist and United Reformed Church as well as a community centre. The present church was built in 1916 and replaced an older 18th Century chapel. Just on from The Ginnel is the **Devonshire Hotel,** a well-proportioned three-storey Georgian house built in about 1730 as a mansion house for Lord Burlington. In 1753 the house became the property of the Dukes of Devonshire and by the end of the 18th Century it had become a coaching inn known as the New Inn. Hidden down along **The Ginnel** is the **Friends Meeting House,** built in 1693 following the Toleration Act of 1689 that allowed dissenting Protestants the freedom of worship. George Fox, the founder of the Quakers, visited Skipton on a number of occasions during the early 17th Century. A pleasant riverside path leads past the **Skipton Devonshire Bowling Club,** which was founded in 1875 and occupies the former gardens and stabling of the Devonshire Hotel.

3. *Turn right along the main road bearing round to the right to reach a small roundabout in Caroline Square at the bottom of the High Street. Head up along the left-hand side of the High Street along Sheep Street then where this opens out into the wide market area, turn left through an archway along Hallams Yard and follow this lane down to reach Canal Street.*

The buildings that look up along the High Street across Caroline Square stand on the site of a house where **Thomas Spencer** was born in 1851, the co-founder of Marks and Spencer. Hidden away along **Sheep Street** is the **Old Town Hall**, with a rather grand flight of steps. This originally served as a courthouse and meeting room for the Town Council before the 'new' Town Hall was built, with a lock-up under the building for petty criminals. Note the two stones on either side of the steps that once formed part of the town's stocks. Numerous narrow alleyways and yards lead off the main High Street, a good example of which is **Hallams Yard**. As Skipton flourished as a mill town during the 18th and 19th Centuries there was great demand for new housing, however, land was in short supply and so many of the old yards behind the High Street were in-filled with cottages.

**4.** *Turn left along Canal Street down to reach the road junction beside the canal bridge. Turn left here along Coach Street and follow this down to reach the T-junction with Swadford Street. Turn right across Belmont Bridge then take the lane to the right after the bridge along Belmont Wharf. Follow the canal towpath all the way to reach the swing bridge beside the large mill complex.*

**Springs Branch** (alongside Canal Street) is a short canal that branches off from the Leeds and Liverpool Canal at Belmont Wharf and into the Eller Beck Gorge behind the Castle, and was once used to transport stone from nearby quarries. Our route heads down along **Coach Street** with its many enticing cobbled alleyways and a small square leading down to the canal complete with old warehouses, then crosses the canal by way of Belmont Bridge and heads along **Belmont Wharf** in the heart of 19th Century 'industrial' Skipton. The **Leeds and Liverpool Canal** stands as Britain's longest inland waterway, an amazing feat of engineering that stretches 127 miles with 91 locks. The canal took 46 years to complete and was opened fully in 1816, although the section from Leeds to Skipton was opened in the 1770's. Freight traffic ceased in the 1960's and the canal is now used by pleasure craft. The arrival of the canal heralded a new era for the town as the once small cottage industries of weaving and wool combing were transformed with quicker access to new markets. Soon large textile mills, warehouses and terraced houses were built alongside the canal. Our route passes an impressive old weaving mill of 1847, which has recently been converted into apartments. The large mill complex down to the left of the swing bridge is **Belle Vue Mills,** otherwise known as Dewhurst's Mill, which dates back to 1828, although rebuilt following a fire in 1831. For over 150 years this was the home of J. Dewhurst & Sons Ltd, who produced high quality cotton sewing threads. It is still a working mill and now produces greetings cards.

**5.** *Turn right across the Swing Bridge and follow Brook Street up to the right to reach Gargrave Road, where you turn right down to a mini-roundabout. Turn right here along Coach Street then head left just before the canal bridge and follow the canal tow-path until you reach the next canal bridge where you head up the steps onto Raikes Road. Follow the road (Mill Bridge) back up into the High Street.*

**Ermysted's Grammar School** was founded as a Free Grammar School in 1492 by an endowment in the will of Peter Toller, the Dean of Craven. The school is, however, named after William Ermysted, the Canon of St Paul's, London, who was a generous benefactor in the 16th Century. This school moved to its present site in 1877. Our route joins the Springs Branch canal beside **Cresap Gardens,** dedicated to Thomas Cresap, a local man who was born at Skipton in 1695 and later established the settlement of Skipton in Maryland, USA on the 'Wild West' frontier. From the second canal bridge along the Springs Branch, there is a wonderful short walk straight on along the canal tow-path through the dramatic **Eller Beck Gorge** behind the Castle. This is a delightful walk that leads to the head of the canal passing a waterfall where the overflow from the old millpond tumbles into the stream. **Chapel Hill** lies just across from Mill Bridge, the site of the original settlement where the old road crossed Eller Beck by way of a ford. In 1764 John Wesley preached in the small square beside the row of old stone cottages. Standing proudly on the hill is the **Old Chapel,** formerly a Methodist Church that was built in 1811 on the site of an earlier chapel of 1791; it has recently been converted into a house. To your right is the **High Corn Mill,** an ancient mill that dates back to medieval times where local farmers brought their grain for milling. The mill is now home to a variety of shops and offices, although its old waterwheel can be clearly seen from the canal tow-path.

# Stokesley

**TIME:** One & a half hours

**START:** The Town Hall overlooking The Plain.

**TOILETS:** Next to the Police Station

**CAFÉ:** Plenty of choice in the town centre.

**PUBS:** Several pubs to choose from; try the Spread Eagle along the High Street or the White Swan along West End.

**PARKING:** Parking in College Square.

**INFORMATION:** Tourist Information Centres: Northallerton 01609 776864 or Great Ayton 01642 722835.

**MARKET DAY:** Friday

> *"Of particular delight are the numerous Georgian houses that line the High Street, their haphazard roofs and chimneys creating an irregular but attractive skyline."*

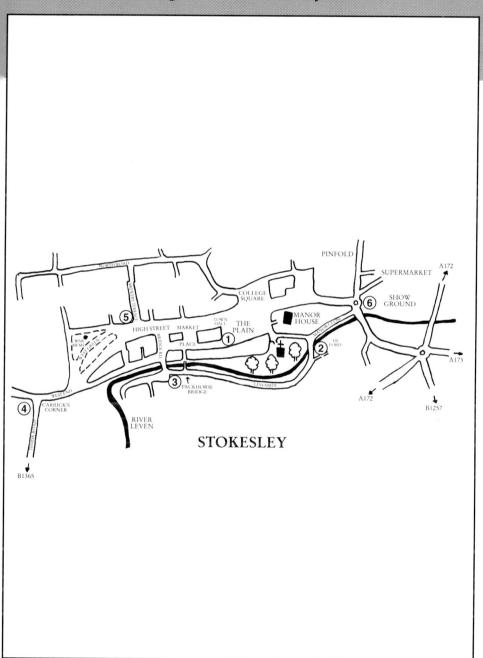

STOKESLEY

**1.** *From the Town Hall bear to the right across The Plain then along a lane out of the top right-hand corner that quickly leads to the Church. A footpath leads to the left through the churchyard (Signpost 'River Leven') and down to reach a footbridge and ford over the river.*

Stokesley can trace its history back over 1,000 years when a Saxon farmer made a clearing in the forest; indeed 'stokes' means wood and 'ley' means a clearing. The settlement developed into a small village complete with a church by the time of the Norman Conquest following which the Lordship of Stokesley was given to Guy de Balliol in the early 12th Century, whose descendants went on to great things including the foundation of Balliol College, Oxford as well as a King of Scotland! This wonderful North Riding market town has served the needs of the district of Cleveland for centuries and is still a thriving place. Of particular delight are the numerous Georgian houses that line the High Street, their haphazard roofs and chimneys creating an irregular but attractive skyline. The imposing grey-stone **Town Hall** was built in 1853 on the site of a former Toll Booth and overlooks **The Plain** where weekly markets are still held; note the ornate clock which commemorates the Queen's Silver Jubilee. Directly across The Plain stands the old **Manor House,** which now houses the town library as well as other Council offices. The Manor House can trace its history back to medieval times when it belonged to the powerful de Balliol family and is said to stand on the site of a castle or fortified house, however it was completely rebuilt in the 18th Century. Sadly much of the building was pulled down following the Second World War. Note the ornately carved gateposts that came from Angrove Hall, which stood to the north east of the town before it was demolished in 1832. The **Church of St Peter and St Paul** stands on a site that has been used for worship since at least the 11th Century. In the 12th Century Guy de Balliol gave the Church as well as some land to St Mary's Abbey at York for the monks to pray for his soul; this stayed in their possession until the Dissolution of the Monasteries. The church was almost entirely rebuilt in the 18th Century to accommodate the expanding population of the town although the chancel and tower date from the 14th Century, their older stonework easily identifiable. It is said that local people sought refuge in the stoutly built tower from Scottish raiders and that weapons were stored there in the 16th Century when the threat of invasion from the Spanish Armada was imminent. The interior is noted for its striking red and green roof, 'Mousey' Thompson furniture and a tapestry depicting the Ruins of Ypres.

**2.** *Cross the footbridge and follow the road (Levenside) alongside the river to your right all the way down passing the stone Packhorse Bridge to reach the Iron Bridge.*

The diminutive **River Leven** flows behind the High Street with trees, grassy verges, old houses and plenty of noisy ducks creating an almost rural scene. Many of the trees were planted in 1935 in remembrance of **Miss Jane Pace** who was born in Stokesley in 1817 and became the first white woman to settle permanently in Victoria, Australia. As you walk down along **Levenside** there are many houses of note including the **Old**

**Rectory,** which is set back behind a high wall, then a row of 17th Century cottages that have been greatly altered over the years. Several imposing houses and old farms are passed before we reach the attractive 17th Century **Packhorse Bridge,** once the only 'dry' crossing of the river that carried the main road into the town from the south. Note the fine brick-built **Preston House** on the left that has associations with John Preston, founder of the Preston Grammar School, near to which stands the **Bethel Chapel** built in 1809. The road opens out at the **Iron Bridge,** built in the late 19th Century when this riverside area began to expand as the 'industrial' heart of the town, hence the numerous river crossings. The large mill complex on the left was built in the early 19th Century as a linen mill, later becoming a corn mill and now home to Armstrong Richardson. Note the cottage near the bridge with its date-stone of 1715 - this would originally have been a humble cottage later raised to two storeys.

*3. Cross the Iron Bridge and head straight up to reach the High Street, where you turn left and follow the High Street until it opens out into West Green. Continue along the road skirting to the left around the perimeter of the Green then head out along West End road until you reach the junction with the Thirsk Road at Carrick's Corner.*
One of the finest buildings in Stokesley lies on the left after the Iron Bridge, a wonderful brick-built Georgian house known as **Red House,** which was restored in 1982. Further towards the High Street on the right is the **Police Station,** a stone building complete with barred windows that dates from the 19th Century when it was built as a Police Station and 'lock-up' for the more unruly inhabitants of the town! **West Green** is a delightful area of residential houses with an almost 'village green' feel about it. An old lane known as **Leven Wynd** leads down to the river around which are many fine Georgian houses with cobbled forecourts looking out across West Green. Of particular note is the **White House,** a Georgian building where John Wesley stayed during one of his many preaching visits to the town during the late 18th Century. The house was also the home of Lady Hullock whose will set up Lady Hullock's Charity in 1854, which provided for the poor of the town. The **White Swan** is an early 18th Century coaching inn, whose old stabling block has recently been converted into a small brewery known as the Captain Cook Brewery, named after the world-famous explorer who was born near Middlesborough and went to school at Great Ayton. The pub is particularly noted for its superb award-winning ploughman's lunches as well as its home-brewed ales. A short detour out along the road known as **West End** takes us past **Oaklands Terrace,** a row of 18th Century cottages where local artist and historian Alec Wright once lived, down to reach an impressive house at the road junction. This is **Oaklands House,** now a nursing home, a wonderful three-storey early Victorian mansion built for a local printer and later occupied by a solicitor called Carrick, hence the name of the road junction. Across the road is a row of four elegant Georgian houses, with exquisite features including typical fan-shaped window lights above the doors.

_Van A. Ivs<sup>?</sup> 01._

4. _Head back along West End to reach West Green and follow the pavement keeping on the left-hand side of the road as it sweeps around West Green. As you join the High Street again, take a detour to the left along Brewery Terrace immediately after the Old Post Office._

**West Green** has some of Stokesley's finest houses including No.62, a superb brick-built house known as **Handyside** with two protruding gables and two symmetrical doors. After Handyside there are a number of very old houses including another which appears to have begun life as a single-storey cottage. No.44 boasts some very fine bow windows, as does No.2 - what is striking is that every house is different and yet they seem to blend together perfectly. As you join the High Street note the **Old Post Office,** complete with inscribed stone Victorian letterbox. **Brewery Terrace** is a good example of what a Victorian yard would have looked like with cobbles and flagged paving, a mixture of old cottages set at angles to each other and then a row of six Georgian cottages. The large house at the end is known as Brewery House and once belonged to the old **Cleveland Brewery** whose brewhouse was situated nearby. At one time every town would have had its own brewery, however this brewery closed around fifty years ago. Incidentally, before it was used as a brewery, Brewery House ironically formed part of a Methodist Chapel in the early 19th Century ago. Retrace your steps back down to the High Street.

**5.** *At the High Street turn left and follow it all the way down to College Square. Continue across the Square passing Preston Grammar School and out along the main road to reach the roundabout near a supermarket.*

There were once numerous inns along this part of the High Street dating from when the town developed as a stop on the old coaching routes, at one time there were over a score of pubs in the town however all but a handful have closed. Continue along the High Street passing the imposing **Methodist Church** to reach **Barclay's Bank,** which is housed in one of the town's architectural gems. This elegant Georgian house was once the home of Dr Yeoman, the town's first Medical Officer of Health. The cobbled area across the road to the left of the Police Station was the site of the old **Market Cross,** which was destroyed in 1783, as well as the old shambles where local butchers had their 'shammels' or meat stalls. The High Street soon opens out into The Plain and **College Square** - note the many old-fashioned and individual shops including butchers, jewellers and bookshops. A small stone building set amongst the group of houses in the middle of College Square was once the **Preston Grammar School.** This was the first grammar school in the town established in 1805 with money bequeathed by John Preston, a local attorney. The present building dates from 1832 and was in use until the Great War; it is now used as a food takeaway outlet.

**6.** *At the roundabout turn right to quickly reach the bridge over the River Leven, immediately before which turn right again along Manor Close down alongside the river. At the footbridge / ford bear right along the footpath through the churchyard back to reach the Town Hall.*

A short detour to the left at the roundabout will quickly bring you to the New Inn pub, across the road from which is The Pound, or **Pinfold.** At one time every village and town would have a pinfold, where stray animals were impounded by the Pindar, only released upon payment of a fine. The large open field directly ahead of you at the roundabout is the Show Ground where the **Stokesley Agricultural Show** has been held since 1859, one of the largest country shows in the North. Beside the road bridge is a preserved **waterwheel** that dates from around 1850, a reminder of a proud history of milling that goes back to the Norman Conquest when Stokesley Mill was recorded in the Domesday Book. Sadly, the old mill buildings were demolished in 1983.

# Thirsk & Sowerby

## ⓘ ESSENTIAL WALK INFORMATION

**TIME:** Two hours

**START:** Thirsk Market Place.

**TOILETS:** Market Place and Millgate car park

**CAFÉ:** Several to choose from in the centre of Thirsk; try Yorks Tea Rooms in the Market Place or George Tempests Café along Kirkgate.

**PUBS:** Plenty of choice - try Ye Olde Three Tuns on Finkle Street, the Blacksmiths Arms in the Market Place, Lord Nelson on St James' Green or the Crown & Anchor at Sowerby.

**PARKING:** The Market Place offers ample parking, there is also a large car park off Millgate.

**INFORMATION:** Thirsk Tourist Information Centre: 01845 522755

**MARKET DAYS:** Monday and Saturday.

*"Thirsk's most famous house stands at 23 Kirkgate. This was the veterinary practice of D. V. Sinclair and J. A. Wight, otherwise known as 'Farnon & Herriot'."*

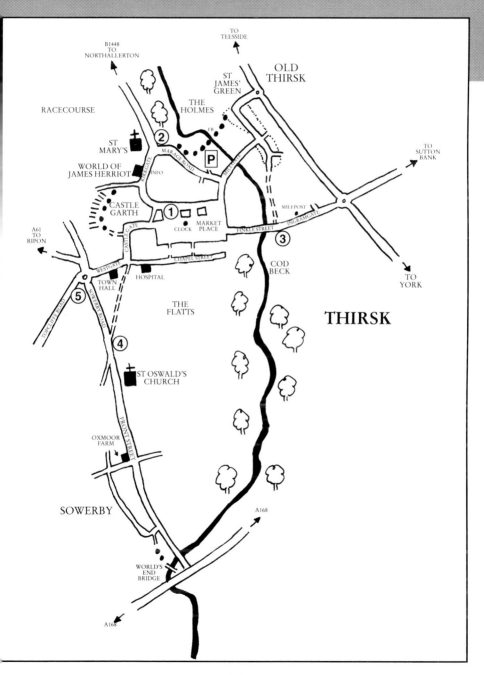

151

**1.** *Leave the Market Place along the Northallerton Road and walk along Kirkgate to reach the St Mary's Church.*

Thirsk is a picturesque, thriving market town situated amongst the rich fields of the Vale of Mowbray with the Hambleton Hills rising to the east. The focal point of the large **Market Place** is the ornate **Clock Tower,** built in 1896 on the site of the ancient market cross to commemorate the marriage of King George V with Princess Mary. Look out for the large iron bull-ring that can still be found set into the cobbles in between the Clock Tower and the Northallerton Road, where bulls were tethered and baited by dogs centuries ago. There are many interesting alleyways leading off the Market Place and Millgate with shops that are no longer found on many high streets including ironmongers, family butchers, bakers and some excellent fish and chip shops. Take a moment to look at the variety of buildings - not one is the same. This corner of the Market Place around Kirkgate retains many original and interesting shops including **Johnson's Butchers Shop,** where they have been making their prize-winning sausages and pies since 1830. The **Darrowby Inn** used to be known as The Red Bear but has been renamed after the town made famous by James Herriot; it is reputedly haunted and has very large cellars that extend out underneath the Market Place. **Bakers Alley** is a stone flagged thoroughfare with many old cottages, named after **John Gilbert Baker** (1834 - 1920) who became the curator of the Royal Botanical Gardens at Kew and lived in a house that once stood at the end of this alley. At 16 Kirkgate is the **Thirsk Museum** which houses a fascinating collection of local artefacts, photographs and displays including the Busby Stoop Chair, which brings misfortune to anyone who sits in it - beware if you're feeling tired! **Thomas Lord** was born in this house in 1755 and later became a famous cricketer. He was employed at the White Conduit Club as a bowler and general attendant when he realised the commercial potential of cricket and decided to start a private ground on land leased at Marylebone in 1787. When the lease ended he literally moved his turf to Regents Park and then to St Johns Wood in 1813, which became known as Lord's Cricket Ground. Thirsk's most famous house stands at 23 Kirkgate. This was the veterinary practice of D. V. Sinclair and J. A. Wight, otherwise known as 'Farnon & Herriot'. Hambleton District Council bought this house following the sad death of Alf Wight, author of the James Herriot books, in 1995 and opened **The World of James Herriot** some four years later. The Museum brings the life and times of this world famous vet vividly to life as this is the actual surgery of Alf Wight and Donald Sinclair and has been carefully developed to look like it would have done fifty years ago as 'Skeldale House' depicted in the books. The Herriot books brought the beauty of the Yorkshire Dales and North York Moors to millions of people worldwide and the Thirsk area is known as 'Herriot Country'. Opposite here is a fine brick-built Victorian tower brewery built in 1863, where the raw ingredients went in at the top and beer came out of the bottom! You soon pass the rather grand Georgian house of **Thirsk Hall,** home of the Bell family since the 18th Century when they also became Lords of the Manor; it is thought that the famous Yorkshire architect John Carr enlarged the house in the late

18th Century. **St Mary's Church** is acclaimed by many as the finest parish church in the North of England and is a stunning example of Perpendicular Gothic architecture, its 88-ft tower dominating the town's skyline. The site has been a place of worship since Saxon times however the present church dates from the early 15th Century and thankfully did not suffer at the hands of the Victorian 'restorers'. The church has many fascinating features including a bell dated 1410 that originally came from Fountains Abbey. The medieval oak roof has many unusual carved bosses, and the South Door is the original oak door which interestingly has a smaller inset door that allowed parishioners to enter rather than local wandering sheep. There are also the faded remains of 17th Century wall paintings, a medieval screen and a window with beautiful medieval stained glass.

2. *At the church turn right along Marage Road down towards the car park, however forsake this road almost immediately for the footpath beside Cod Beck. Follow this riverside path down over a footbridge and up to reach St James' Green. Turn right and walk across St James' Green, over Bridge Street then continue across the Green and out of the far bottom right-hand corner along a track that leads down to a riverside path and on to the road bridge.*

People have been living in this area since prehistoric times, however 'Tresche' was first mentioned in the Domesday Book. Its name is somewhat of a rarity as it is derived from an old Celtic word meaning 'place by the water' - most placenames are either

Scandinavian or Anglo-Saxon. The area beside **Cod Beck** is known as **The Holmes** and is an area of common land with many old willow trees; 'coed' is ancient British for 'wood'. A mill race once ran alongside Cod Beck and provided power for a 19th Century corn and flour mill that stood beside the old stone bridge along Millgate where the car park is now. **St James' Green** is in 'Old Thirsk' and has many fine two and three-storey red brick buildings, including some delightful Georgian houses. A short detour to the left along **Ingramgate** at the road bridge over Cod Beck takes you to an unusual milepost with the image of a man with a walking stick and what looks like a pint of ale; this figure is used as the emblem of Thirsk Museum. From the road bridge look downstream to see the remains of the moorings that were meant to be for the ambitious **Thirsk Canal Scheme.** In 1767 attempts were made to make Cod Beck navigable to the River Swale, however lack of money meant that the scheme was abandoned.

**3.** *Turn right over the bridge and follow Finkle Street back up into the Market Place, then turn left through the archway to the left of the Golden Fleece and walk through the yard to join Chapel Street. Turn right and follow this lane up passing the Lambert Memorial Hospital to reach the junction with Castlegate, where you turn left along a wide footpath that leads past a play area (The Flatts are to your left) to reach Sowerby Road.*

Thirsk lies at the crossroads of several busy routes north and east and became an important staging post during the 18th Century between London, York and the North and a number of fine old coaching inns still line the Market Place. **The Three Tuns Hotel** is a fine 18th Century house originally built for the Bell family and retains a wonderful sweeping staircase. The **Golden Fleece** dominates the Market Place as it has done for over 200 years and has an elegant charm about it reminiscent of days gone by. Behind these two old inns are the remains of the old stabling blocks. **The Blacksmiths Arms** dates back to the 14th Century and was reputedly built by the same craftsmen that built the Merchant Adventurers Hall at York. It is certainly an inn of great character with slanting walls, wood panelling and low beams as well as a resident ghost. In the heyday of the coaching era there was a blacksmiths' shop to the rear of this pub. The town once supported 30 pubs and four breweries - no wonder it was a popular overnight stop! **Lambert Memorial Hospital** is a small cottage hospital that has served the town since 1890 when it was established by Mrs Lambert in memory of her late husband, Dr Lambert. The area of open common land between Thirsk and Sowerby is known as The Flatts and provides the residents of this area with an 'oasis' of greenery right in the heart of the town with views of the Hambleton Hills stretching away into the distance.

**4.** *Turn left along the main road through Sowerby passing St Oswald's Church down to the end of the village. Retrace your steps back through the village following the main road all the way to reach the roundabout where Sowerby Road meets Westgate.*

**Sowerby** retains its own separate identity away from its close neighbour, indeed this has always been a separate village since it was first settled by a Danish farmer in the 10th Century literally on the doorstep of the older settlement of Thirsk. **St Oswald's Church** was almost completely 'restored' during the 19th Century although an ornate Norman doorway remains intact with inscriptions dated 1680 and 1739 etched onto the wooden door -could this be some of the earliest vandalism in the country? Behind the **Old Manor House,** which stands on the site of a medieval manor house, is a complete group of old farm buildings with a wonderful example of a brick-built Dove Cote. The lovely tree-lined street through Sowerby is lined with tiny cottages, terraced houses, old farms and mansions - an amazing assortment of houses all of different sizes, shapes, styles and periods but all of the same brick type. On the corner of Gravel Hole Lane is an ancient timber-framed cottage known as **Oxmoor Farm,** the oldest building in the area. At the very bottom of the village to the right of the modern road bridge is a small 17th Century packhorse bridge over Cod Beck known as **World's End Bridge,** which was once the main route into the village. As you walk back towards Thirsk along **Sowerby Road** you pass a row of small terraced houses each with different coloured window ledges - perhaps this is to help the residents identify their houses easily!

**5.** *Turn right down Westgate and follow the road round to the left along Castlegate, however where this road bends round to the right towards the Market Place take the alley up to the left after Lee's Butchers Shop. Follow the path up to quickly reach Castle Garth, then head to the right across the open field to a gate that leads onto Masonic Lane (with the tower of St Mary's Church in the distance). Turn right here right down to reach Kirkgate where you head right back into the Market Place.*

At the junction with Westgate stands a house overlooking a cobbled square where **George Macauley** was born in 1897. George played cricket for Yorkshire and England taking 1,733 wickets for his county as well as scoring 5,759 runs. He was famous for taking a wicket with his very first ball of his very first Test Match! As you walk along Westgate note the old **County Police Station** and **Court House** on the right and the old fashioned **Ritz Cinema,** which opened in the early 1900's. The large building on the corner where Westgate turns to the left into Castlegate was formerly a branch of the Yorkshire Penny Bank, however it closed about twenty years ago and is now 'The Mind Shop'. The field known as **Castle Garth** was once the site of **Thirsk Castle.** In 1092 Robert de Stuteville built a wooden Norman castle on land he had been granted by William the Conqueror. However, in 1174 Roger de Mowbray held the castle during an unsuccessful revolt against Henry II and it was reduced to ashes in the following year; all that remains is a ditch and mound in the field. Recent excavations have revealed that this site had previously been used as a Saxon burial ground in the 7th Century.

# Whitby

**TIME:** Three hours

**START:** The Swing Bridge across the Harbour.

**TOILETS:** Langborne Road or in the Market Place.

**PARKING:** Large car parks off Langborne Road beside the Station.

**CAFÉ:** Spoilt for choice; for fish and chips try Hadley's Fish Restaurant along Bridge Street or the Magpie Café along Pier Road; for a café try the Whitby Tea Rooms or Abbey Steps Tea Room along Church Street.

**PUBS:** Plenty of choice; try the Black Horse along Church Street or the Little Angel Inn along St Hilda's Terrace.

**INFORMATION:** Whitby Tourist Information Centre: 01947 602674

**MARKET DAYS:** Tuesday and Saturday.

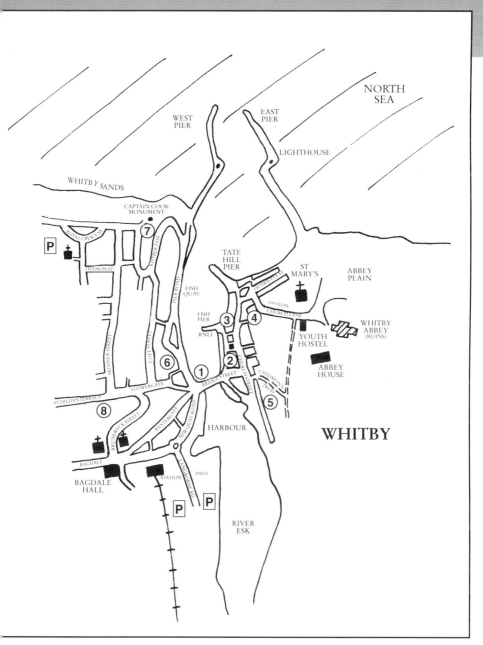

**1.** *From the Swing Bridge across the Harbour in the centre of Whitby head up along Bridge Street towards Whitby Abbey then, as the road swings round to the right, turn left along Church Street and follow this lane to where the Market Place opens out on your left.*

A sense of excitement and adventure fills the air as you enter Whitby as this bustling seaside resort and fishing port was where wooden sailing ships once set sail on whaling expeditions and Captain Cook embarked on his many famous journeys of discovery. The Old Town of Whitby lies on the 'east' side, a jumble of narrow streets and old cottages clinging to the cliff beneath the ruins of Whitby Abbey. **Church Street** runs through the heart of the old town with many fine old shops and houses lining the cobbled lane. Buildings of note include the **White Horse and Griffin**, a lovely old coaching inn with a wonderful façade, where Charles Dickens once stayed and Captain Cook reputedly met shipbuilders to discuss his voyages - the first stagecoach from Whitby to York set off from White Horse Yard in 1788. Further along Church Street is the **Black Horse** pub, another old coaching inn that was originally called the White Horse but changed its name to avoid confusion; the present building dates from around 1823. Black Horse Yard leads to the side of this pub, a fine cobbled courtyard where the kitchen midden, or rubbish tip, of St Hilda's Abbey was discovered in the 19th Century with artefacts such as a 7th Century lead seal from Rome being unearthed.

**2.** *Turn left through the Market Place and follow the lane out of the bottom right-hand corner down to reach Fish Pier. Retrace your steps, however, just before you reach the Market Place again turn left along a narrow lane (Brewster Lane) back up to Church Street.*

The small **Market Square** was laid out in 1640 by Sir Hugh Cholmley, the Lord of the Manor whose family had bought the abbey estates following the Dissolution of the Monasteries, to replace the old market that had been held in Golden Lion Yard across the Swing Bridge. The **Town Hall** was built in 1788 by Nathaniel Cholmley, whose Coat of Arms can be seen on the side of the building. This elegant stone building with its columns and veranda once served as the dairy market and boasts a fine clock tower surmounted by a golden fish! **Sandgate** leads out of the bottom left-hand corner of the Market Place, where you will find a wealth of small gift shops. This was originally the site of the town's Shambles, or butcher's shops - one or two of the old shop-fronts remain. Fresh fish was brought up to be sold in this market from **Fish Pier**, which was built in the 17th Century and served as the quay for fishing boats until the new quayside was built on the 'west' side of the Harbour. It was during the 18th Century that Whitby began to develop as a centre for shipbuilding, fishing and whaling and before long the town was the seventh most important port in the country. Between 1753 and the 1830's numerous whaling ships set sail from here for Arctic waters, the whale blubber being rendered on the quayside into oil which was used as fuel for the town's streetlights, as well as being sold for other uses further afield. Here you will find the **RNLI Lifeboat Station** with its large 'Trent Class' Lifeboat - there has been a Lifeboat Station at Whitby since 1802.

**3.** *Turn left along Church Street then where the road turns sharply round to the right towards the bottom of Church Stairs take the lane off to the left down along Tate Hill. Follow this lane down passing Tate Hill Pier on your left then up and round to the right along Sandside to reach the bottom of Church Stairs. Turn left here along Henrietta Street until you reach the end of the road and houses, then retrace your steps back to Church Stairs.*

This area of Church Street is a delight with many enticing yards and ghauts (alleys leading to the river) leading off the main street. These yards are often crammed with old cottages, built as the town's population burgeoned during the 18th Century. Further along Church Street is the **Victorian Jet Works,** with its mural depicting the various processes involved in jet working. Here you can see craftsmen at work as well as an authentic Victorian jet workshop dating from 1867. At its height in the 1870's there were 200 workshops and over 1,400 people employed in the jet industry, however there are now only a handful of shops. Jet is the fossilised remains of the monkey puzzle tree and is only found along this stretch of coastline. Although Jet has been collected and polished for centuries, the Jet Industry began in earnest during the 19th Century and became fashionable after the death of Prince Albert when Queen Victoria wore it as her 'mourning' jewellery. **Tate Hill Pier** is Whitby's oldest pier that dates back to 1545, the construction of which turned the river estuary into a harbour. This was also where, in Bram Stoker's 'Dracula', the Russian schooner Demeter crashed into the pier and Count Dracula, in the form of a black dog, leapt ashore and disappeared into the darkness - Bram Stoker stayed in the town during the 1890's and gained inspiration for his famous novel from the narrow streets and ruined cliff-top abbey. **Henrietta Street** was once the home of wealthy shipowners, however a cliff-fall in 1787 destroyed many of the houses. Tucked away at the end of this street is the tiny smokehouse of **Fortune's Whitby Cured Kippers,** who have been producing their world-famous kippers here since 1872.

**4.** *Climb up Church Stairs to St Mary's Church, then walk through the churchyard to reach Whitby Abbey. Walk back towards the Church along the cobbled lane that runs parallel to Church Stairs, then immediately after the Youth Hostel turn left along a path - do not head down along the cobbled road. Follow this footpath straight on with the stone wall on your left and open fields on your right then, just before the houses on the right, turn right along a path (Caedmons Trod) that leads down steps to reach Church Street.*

**Church Stairs,** with its famous 199 steps, dates back to at least 1390 and was originally wooden, hence 'stairs' and not 'steps' - the flat areas were once used by pall-bearers to rest coffins on. **Caedmons Cross,** a finely carved Celtic cross, stands at the tops of Church Stairs, erected in 1898 to commemorate Caedmon who wrote the first hymns and poems in English in the 7th Century and thus gave birth to English Literature. Caedmon was a local herdsman who was given the ability to compose songs by an angel who visited him in a dream. St Hilda learnt of this 'miracle' and took him into the monastery where he spent the rest of his life as a monk. **St Mary's Church** stands as one of the most amazing parish churches in England. Built in the early 12th Century by Abbot William de Percy, much of the original Norman church remains although alterations were made in the Georgian period. The church is noted for its amazing array of Georgian galleries and pews that can accommodate over 1,500 worshippers. Note the memorial to Francis and Mary Huntrodds who were born on the same day in 1600, married on their birthdays and both died on the same day aged 80 *"So fit a match, surely, could never be, both in their lives and in their deaths agree."* **Whitby Abbey**, or Streonshalh as it was known then, was founded by King Oswy of Northumbria in 657AD. St Hilda was its first abbess and she established a double monastery of nuns and monks. It was here in 663AD that the Synod of Whitby determined the future organisation of the Church in this country when it decided to follow the Roman instead of the Celtic tradition and also decided the dates of Easter. This abbey was destroyed by Viking raiders in the 9th Century and lay in ruins until after the Norman Conquest. In 1078 a new Benedictine Abbey rose from the ruins, although the present abbey dates from the rebuilding of 1220. Following Henry VIII's Dissolution of the Monasteries in the 16th Century, the roofs were stripped of lead and the buildings plundered.

**5.** *Turn left along Church Street then take the first turning on the right along Grape Lane that leads back to Bridge Street and the Swing Bridge. Walk over the bridge and head straight on across the main road and up through the small 'square' between the bank and the old Customs House (Golden Lion Yard). Follow the lane steeply up (Golden Lion Bank) to reach the bottom of Flowergate, forsake this road for the alleyway (St Anne's Lane) that leads out of the bottom corner of Flowergate down to reach quayside.*

As you reach Church Street again, note the three-storey timber framed house opposite that was built in 1390 for a wealthy merchant, to the left of which is a row of 17th Century cottages with overhanging eaves. **Grape Lane**, originally called Grope Lane as it was unlit, boasts many buildings of interest including a fine red house with the inscription '1688 MDS'. This was where Captain James Cook lodged and studied between 1746 and 1749 when he was apprenticed to John Walker, a wealthy Quaker shipowner; it is now a museum. There has been a bridge across the River Esk at this point since the early 14th Century. The present bridge, with its unique swinging sections to allow vessels into the Upper Harbour, was opened in 1909. The small 'square' across from the **Swing Bridge** is known as **Golden Lion Yard** and takes its name from the very small old pub on the steep lane. This was the site of the original market place prior to 1640. **Flowergate** is lined with attractive 18th Century houses, at the bottom of which is the **Sutcliffe Gallery**, where you can buy prints of the work of the famous Victorian photographer Frank Sutcliffe (1853 - 1941), whose sepia images of Whitby have captured a lost age.

**6.** *Turn left and follow the road round to the left then right along Haggersgate then just before the road opens out as you approach the Fish Quay, turn left up a flight of steps (Pier Lane) that lead up to Cliff Street. Turn right along Cliff Street to reach a road junction (Khyber Pass), where you head straight over the road and up across the gardens onto East Terrace. Turn right along the road to reach the Captain Cook Monument.*

**Haggersgate** originally fronted the harbour before new quays were built in the 18th Century. Tucked away along this street is **Haggersgate House,** a wonderful early Georgian house built for the Yeoman family, who were master mariners and shipowners in the town for several generations. It is now used by the Whitby Mission and Seafarer's Trust. Haggersgate leads down to Fish Quay at the heart of the working port, however our route turns up along a passageway known as Pier Lane that leads up onto **Cliff Street,** with its lovely 17th Century and Georgian properties. Cliff Street, as the name suggests, originally led from the heart of the town out onto the open fields above the West Cliff. In 1845 George Hudson (the 'Railway King') bought much of this area, known as West Fields, as he had recently purchased the Whitby to Pickering Railway and saw an opportunity to develop Whitby as a coastal resort and 'spa' town. The **West Cliff** area became known as the New Town as rows of sweeping terraces were built during the 1850's. The exotically named **Khyber Pass** road was cut through the rock in 1848 to provide quicker access to the Harbour. The **Captain Cook Monument** looks out across the Old Town towards the North Sea, a tribute to one of the world's most famous explorers who set sail from Whitby during the late 18th Century on three of the greatest voyages of exploration of all time. Nearby is an archway made from the jawbones of a whale, a reminder of this once flourishing industry.

**7.** *Follow the main road round to the left along West Cliff then take the second turning on your left along Royal Crescent and follow this curving street down then take the first turning to the left along Crescent Avenue. Head straight on then turn left along Hudson Street, at the end of which turn right along Belle Vue Terrace / Havelock Place which leads onto Skinner Street down to reach a junction with St Hilda's Terrace.*

**Royal Crescent** forms the centrepiece of Hudson's New Town, a wonderful sweeping row of elegant houses, however only half of the crescent was completed as the developer ran out of money due to a financial scandal in 1859 that saw the downfall of George Hudson. Number 6 Royal Crescent was where Bram Stoker stayed. **Skinner Street** is lined with many lovely old-fashioned shops, many of which have retained their original façades including Elizabeth Botham & Sons, confectioners and bakers, a family run business dating back to 1865 that is renowned for their cakes, pastries and plum bread.

**8.** *Turn left along St Hilda's Terrace then follow the road down to the right along Brunswick Street to reach Victoria Square at the junction of Bagdale and Baxtergate. Walk to the left along Baxtergate then take the first turning to the right along Wellington Road to reach the Railway Station. Turn left through Station Square and along New Quay Road back to the Swing Bridge.*

**St Hilda's Terrace** was laid out in the late 18th Century for wealthy shipowners and captains and is lined with ornate Georgian houses that overlook Pannett Park, home of the Art Gallery and Whitby Museum. The **Little Angel Inn** is a lovely old-fashioned pub, parts of which date back to medieval times. At the bottom of Brunswick Street is **Bagdale Hall,** which was built in the early 16th Century for James Conyers, Sergeant at Arms to Henry VIII, and was later the home of Captain Browne Bushell who was executed for treason in 1651 after changing sides several times during the Civil War. **Baxtergate** originally bordered the river estuary with many of the houses built upon sandbanks. Just along from the turning into Wellington Road is the **Old Smuggler Café,** formerly an inn known as the Ship Launch Inn that dates back to 1401 and was once the haunt of shipbuilders and smugglers. The figurehead on the wall is said to have come from a smuggler's ship and put there by Customs and Excise as a deterrent! The elegant stone-built **Station** opened in 1847 and forms the terminus of the scenic Esk Valley Railway. The Whitby to Pickering Railway opened in 1836 to provide a stimulus for the town's flagging whaling and shipbuilding industries - the original station was further up the harbour. Designed by George Stephenson, the 'Father of the Railways', this railway was originally horse-drawn, however George Hudson bought the line in 1845 and set about upgrading and extending it. The area between the Station and the river once formed part of the Harbour and was the site of numerous shipyards during the 18th Century where Captain Cook's ship 'Endeavour' was built. A focal point for this area is the **Crow's Nest** memorial. This monument celebrates the town's seafaring families, in particular the Scoresby family. Captain William Scoresby embarked on many journeys out of Whitby and became one of the most prolific whaling captains in Europe, introducing many revolutionary ideas to improve his whaling ships including the Crow's Nest which helped spot whales out at sea. In 1806 Scoresby navigated his ship to within 510 miles of the North Pole, closer than any person before him.

# York

**TIME:** Three hours

**START:** York Minster.

**TOILETS:** There are plenty of public toilets in the City Centre including Parliament Street, St Leonard's Place and the Museum Gardens.

**CAFÉS:** Plenty of choice; try Betty's along Davygate or Café Concerto along High Petergate.

**PUBS:** Spoilt for choice; try the Kings Arms beside Ouse Bridge, The Maltings near Lendal Bridge or the Minster Inn along Marygate.

**PARKING:** Numerous car parks surround the city centre including Clarence Street, Lord Mayor's Walk, Clifford's Tower and Tanner Row as well as a Park & Ride scheme at various points along the Ring Road.

**INFORMATION:** York Tourist Information Centre: 01904 621756

**MARKET DAYS:** Monday to Saturday

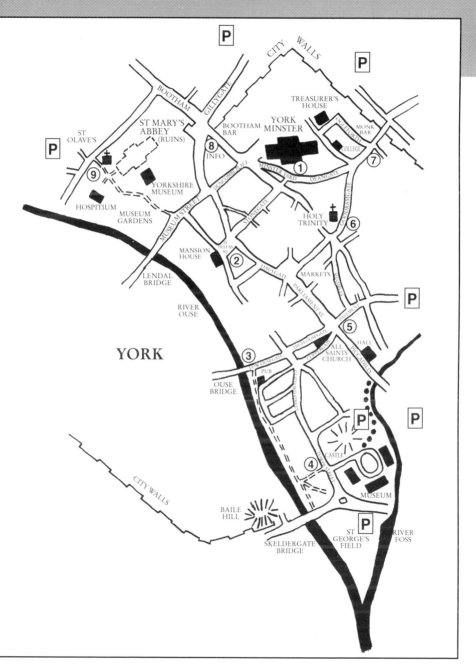

**1.** *From the South Transept of York Minster (beneath the Rose Window) head straight across the road along Minster Gates and continue straight on down Stonegate to reach St Helen's Square.*

The Romans chose the spur of land near the confluence of the rivers Ouse and Foss for their military headquarters and for almost 350 years **Eboracum** was the principal Roman city of Northern Britain. Following their departure in around AD410, the city was taken over by Anglo-Saxon invaders who named it **Eoforwic** then in the 9th Century Vikings captured the city, which became known as **Jorvik**. Following the Norman Conquest a stone castle was built, the city walls strengthened and extended and medieval York developed into a powerful and wealthy city as well as an important port and trading centre. In the 18th Century the city became a fashionable 'social' centre for wealthy people and in the Victorian era York flourished with the arrival of the railways and the rise of the Quaker chocolate families of Terry and Rowntree. These layers of history stretching back 2,000 years are waiting to be discovered; as King George VI said *"The history of York is the history of England"*. **York Minster** stands as the largest Gothic cathedral in Northern Europe, a masterpiece of medieval architecture. The history of the Minster stretches back to 627AD when a small wooden church was built on the site of the Roman Military Headquarters to baptise King Edwin of Northumbria. This Anglo-Saxon church was rebuilt in stone only a few years later, however, following the Norman Conquest in the 11th Century it was replaced by an immense cathedral only to be replaced again by the present Minster which was started in 1220 and finally completed in 1472. York Minster abounds in art treasures including the 15th Century Choir Screen, the Five Sisters Window and the Great East Window that dates from 1405 (the largest expanse of medieval glass in the world). **The South Transept** famously caught fire after it was struck by lightning in 1984 and the resulting blaze destroyed the roof and cracked the 16th Century Rose Window into 30,000 pieces. Following careful restoration the Rose Window has been restored to its former glory. Between 1967 and 1972 the area beneath the Central Tower was excavated and the foundations of the massive stone pillars were encased in concrete to prevent the Tower from collapsing. It was during this excavation that the remains of the Norman Cathedral, Anglo-Saxon church and Roman Headquarters were discovered, which can still be seen in the **Undercroft** and Crypt. Near the South Door is a statue of **Constantine The Great** who was proclaimed Emperor in 306AD in the Military Headquarters of Eboracum; two Roman Emperors died and one was proclaimed at York. His recognition of Christianity as the official religion of the Empire as well as his own conversion to the faith established the religious foundations of Western Christendom. The paved lane of Minster Gates quickly leads across **Petergate**, the 'Via Principalis' or main street of the Roman fortress, and onto Stonegate, which lies on the line of the Roman road of Via Praetoria that led from the Headquarters to the river crossing. **Stonegate** is lined with wonderful medieval buildings, many of which still retain their Georgian and Victorian shop-fronts. Look out for the red **Stonegate Devil,** a carved 'printer's devil' above a former printer's shop. A short detour to the left down along **Coffee Yard** (alleyways are known as Snickleways in York) leads to Barley Hall, a 15th Century medieval townhouse that has been recently restored, whilst further along Stonegate is **Mulberry Hall**, a magnificent timber-framed house built in 1434.

*2. As you walk into St Helen's Square turn left along Davygate and follow this down until it opens out into St Sampson's Square. Continue straight on along what is now Parliament Street then just before you reach the road junction at the bottom of this street, turn right immediately before the Parish Church of All Saints Pavement along High Ousegate. Follow this down to reach the road junction with Spurriergate and Nessgate, where you continue straight on along Low Ousegate to reach Ouse Bridge.*
**St Helen's Square** is dominated by the **Mansion House,** an imposing cream and scarlet house built in 1730 that serves as the residence of the Lord Mayor during their year of office. Set into the pavement in front of the Mansion house are cobbles that mark the line of the Roman wall that surrounded the military fortress of Eboracum, this was also the site of the **Praetorian Gate** or main entrance into the Roman city. **Davygate** soon opens out into **St Sampson's Square** with the Roman Bath pub across to the left, which stands above a large bathhouse once used by Roman soldiers. Markets have been held in this area for centuries, indeed in medieval times houses were even pulled down to make way for more market stalls! Just off **Parliament Street** is **Newgate Market,** a bustling street market set against a backdrop of medieval buildings. York boasts nineteen medieval churches (although there were originally over twice this number), many of which were built by wealthy merchants during the Middle Ages. **The Parish Church of All Saints Pavement** is an ancient guild church, famed for its Lantern Tower, that dates predominantly from the 15th Century, although there may have been a Pre-Conquest church on this site.

*3. Take the steps to the left immediately before Ouse Bridge down onto King's Staith, passing the Kings Arms pub on your left and follow the riverbank straight on to reach the gardens just before Skeldergate Bridge. Turn left through the gardens to reach Clifford's Tower (York Castle).*
York lies at the confluence of two rivers, so it is not surprising that it often floods, despite a flood barrier on the **River Foss.** The famous **Kings Arms** has been flooded on countless occasions - inside the pub is a board that charts the height of the floodwater, the worst (so far) being November 2000 when water almost reached the first floor windows. York has been an important port since Roman times, however its heyday was during the medieval period when products such as wool and lead were exported on boats via the River Ouse and the Humber to Europe. The **King's Staith,** along with **Queen's Staith** across the river, formed the docks of York and many of the old warehouses can still be seen, although they have since been converted into flats and hotels.

**4.** *Walk between Clifford's Tower and the Castle Museum then bear to the left across the car park to join a path alongside the River Foss just to the right of the Coppergate Shopping Centre. Follow this riverside path to reach Piccadilly where you turn left up to reach the bottom of Parliament Street.*

**Clifford's Tower,** properly called the Great Tower, is one of York's most famous landmarks. Following the Norman Conquest a motte and bailey castle was built across the river from the present castle on a mound still known as Baile Hill, however this was destroyed a year later by the people of York who resented their new Norman lords. A 'new' wooden castle was constructed on the land between the Foss and the Ouse and then rebuilt in stone in the mid 13th Century during the reign of Henry III - Clifford's Tower is the only surviving part of this medieval castle. **York Castle** became one of the most important in the country where Kings regularly stayed - medieval York was second only to London. Following the defeat of the Royalist forces during the English Civil War the Castle was used as a prison and then Clifford's Tower was gutted by fire in 1684. Directly across from the Tower is the **Debtors' Prison** built in 1701 on the site of the Castle's bailey which, along with the old **Female Prison** of 1780 to the left, form **York Castle Museum,** the most popular folk museum in the country. The building to the right was built in 1773 as the **York Assize Court** and is still used as a Crown Court. Dick Turpin, the famed highwayman, spent a number of months in the Debtors' Prison before being hanged at York in 1739. The **Merchant Adventurers' Hall** on Piccadilly is the finest surviving medieval guildhall in Europe dating back to 1357, from where the Guild of Merchants conducted their business affairs, met socially, looked after the poor and prayed to God. This Guild dominated the commerce of the city in medieval times creating much of its wealth and employment; a Merchant Adventurer was a trader who risked (hence 'adventurer') his money in overseas trade and so this Guild was established to 'pool' the risk. The Great Hall is a wonderful example of a 14th Century timber-framed building with an incredible oak roof, whilst beneath this is the Undercroft which was used as a hospital from 1373 until 1900 with a small adjoining chapel. The Hall is still in the ownership of the Company of Merchant Adventurers.


**5.** *At the junction at the bottom of Parliament Street turn right along The Pavement then take the first turning to the left into the Shambles. Walk up to the top of this street then turn right and head diagonally across King's Square to reach the crossroads with Goodramgate on your right.*

Markets and public gatherings were once held along **The Pavement,** including the execution of Thomas Percy, Earl of Northumberland, who was beheaded in 1572. Note the fine timbered **Herbert House** on the right where Sir Thomas Herbert was born in 1606, a friend of Charles I who attended the King's execution. **The Shambles** is York's most famous street where the medieval houses are so close together that it is possible to shake hands from the upstairs windows across the street. This is the ancient street of the butchers dating back to Pre-Conquest times and takes its name from the Old English word 'Fleshammels' meaning the stalls on which meat was displayed. You can still see many of the old butchers' shops with their hooks and benches at the front. Situated along the Shambles is the **Shrine of St Margaret of York.** Margaret Clitherow was born at York in 1553 and lived in this house during the Reformation, a period when Catholics were persecuted, bravely she continued to practice the Old Faith and was put on trial in 1586 for harbouring priests and attending mass and sentenced to death. She was canonised in 1970.

**6.** *Turn right along Goodramgate then where this road meets Deangate turn off to the left along College Street with the Minster ahead of you. Head straight on passing St William's College on your right then follow the lane round to the right along Minster Yard then take the turning to the right at the Treasurer's House down along Chapter House Street. Follow this round to the right (now Ogleforth) back to reach Goodramgate.*

**Goodramgate** takes its name from the old Scandinavian personal name of Gutherun and 'gata' the Norse word for a street. An archway to the left leads to **Holy Trinity Church,** one of the finest 'hidden' churches in York that dates back to the 13th Century and remains completely unaltered with an uneven flagged floor and 17th Century box pews. **Ladys Row** backs onto this churchyard, the oldest row of houses in York built in 1316. **St William's College** is situated along College Street, a lovely stone and timbered-framed house built in the 1460's as a residence for the Chantry Priests of the Cathedral. It remained as a college of priests until the Reformation when it passed into private ownership, then in 1902 it became the property of the Dean and Chapter of York Minster. Hidden away off Minster Yard is the **Treasurer's House,** an elegant stone-built house of wonderful proportions that dates largely from the 17th Century. It stands on the site of the medieval house of the Treasurers of the Minster, an office of great power that dates back to the 11th Century, although it was abolished during the Reformation in the 16th Century. The Treasurer's House became the property of the 'new' Protestant Archbishop and was subsequently rebuilt, although it was soon sold into private hands. By the time Frank Green, a wealthy industrialist from Wakefield, bought the house in 1897 it had been converted into three apartments. He was an avid collector of art and furniture and so bought the house as somewhat of a hobby so he could display his many treasures. He restored the house and decorated the different rooms in various period styles ranging from Medieval to Georgian. Frank Green gave the house and its contents to The National Trust in 1930. York is one of the world's most haunted cities with over 140 recorded ghosts and perhaps the most famous story relates to the Treasurer's House. During the 1950's, a man was working in its cellar when he heard the blast of a trumpet and a Roman soldier on horseback marched through the wall followed by a dozen foot soldiers. Excavations later revealed that the Roman road of Via Decumana lay just beneath the floor of the cellar; Chapter House Street follows the line of this ancient road.

**7.** *Turn left along Goodramgate to quickly reach Monk Bar then take the flight of steps through the small doorway set in the Bar (before the archway) that leads up onto the Walls. Turn left and walk along the Walls to reach Bootham Bar where you follow the steps down to street level.*

**Monk Bar** is the tallest of York's four main Bars, or gates, into the walled medieval city. It was built in the 13th Century and still retains its original portcullis in working order - note the small stone figures on top of the Bar, some of which are holding rocks ready to drop on your head! The **City Walls**, properly known as the Bar Walls, still encircle the ancient city and stand as the best preserved medieval walls in the country. They were built in the 13th and 14th Centuries to protect the city from attack, especially from Scottish raids, however some fragments of the original Roman walls still remain. The section of wall from Monk Bar to Bootham Bar was built on the foundations of the Roman walls, indeed **Bootham Bar** stands on the site of the Roman gateway from the north into the military fortress. Unbelievably, moves were made in Victorian times to pull down large sections of the Walls to ease traffic congestion - one section of wall disappeared to make way for **St Leonard's Place** before public opinion prevented more destruction.

John A. Ives '00

**8.** *Cross over St Leonard's Place and head straight on along Bootham passing Exhibition Square on your left. Take the first turning to the left along Marygate and follow this down to reach St Olave's Church. Head through the gate to the left after this church into Museum Gardens.*

The **City Art Gallery** looks out across **Exhibition Square,** built in 1879 for the Fine Art and Industrial Exhibition, to the left of which is **King's Manor,** the former residence of the Abbot of St Mary's Abbey although the original 13th Century house was rebuilt in the late 15th Century. Following Henry VIII's Dissolution of the Monasteries it was used as the Headquarters of the Council of the North until 1641. Many Kings of England have stayed here including James I and Charles I, whose Coat of Arms can be seen above the door. The house has been occupied by the University of York Archaeology Department since 1963. The stone wall that runs alongside Bootham formed part of the **Abbey Walls,** built in the 13th Century to protect St Mary's Abbey, which lay outside the City Walls. The section of wall along Marygate is unique as it retains the grooves in the stonework from where small shutters were hung on hinges to protect archers from a returning flight of arrows. The **Parish Church of St Olave,** dedicated to an early Christian King of Norway called Olaf, was founded in 1050 by Earl Siward of Northumbria but was largely rebuilt in the 18th and 19th Centuries.

**9.** *Walk through the Gardens passing the ruined Abbey and the Yorkshire Museum and on through the elaborate entrance gates onto Museum Street where you turn left back to reach York Minster.*

**St Mary's Abbey** was founded in 1089 by Benedictine monks and grew to become one of the most powerful and wealthy abbeys in the country, however, the buildings were plundered following the Dissolution of the Monasteries in the 16th Century; the ruins we see today date from the 13th Century. The **Hospitium** of St Mary's still stands in the **Museum Gardens,** a 14th Century guest house where travellers to the Abbey would have stayed for the night. Museum Gardens are also home to the **Yorkshire Museum,** with its striking Doric columns and large portico, which houses some of the finest treasures of Yorkshire spanning two millennia with Roman, Viking and medieval artefacts including the famous Middleham Jewel. Just past the Museum is the **Multangular Tower,** the south west corner tower and curtain wall of the Roman fortress dating from around 300AD, a rare survivor indeed although the upper stonework is medieval. The ruined buildings to your left as you reach **Museum Street** are all that remains of **St Leonard's Hospital,** the largest medieval hospital in the North that once extended across Museum Street and St Leonard's Place.

*Other books published by InnWay Publications:*

**The Inn Way...to the English Lake District**
by Mark Reid (ISBN 1 902001 01 X)

**The Inn Way...to the Yorkshire Dales**
by Mark Reid (ISBN 1 902001 03 6)

**The Inn Way...to the North York Moors**
by Mark Reid (ISBN 1 902001 04 4)

**The Inn Way...to Black Sheep Pubs**
by Mark Reid (ISBN 1 902001 02 8)

*For further information please send a SAE to*
*InnWay Publications, 102 Leeds Road, Harrogate, HG2 8HB.*

*InnWay Publications Website*
**www.innway.co.uk**

Printed by Spectrum Print Tel: 01472 340862